Calas

D0707822

PARIS WAS A WOMAN

PARIS was a WOMAN

PORTRAITS FROM THE LEFT BANK

ANDREA WEISS

COUNTERPOINT
BERKELEY

Copyright © 1995, 2013 by Andrea Weiss

All rights reserved under International and Pan-American Copyright Conventions. No part of this book may be used or reproduced in any manner whatsoever without written permission from the publisher, except in the case of brief quotations embodied in critical articles and reviews.

Quotations from *The New Yorker* are reprinted by permission; copyright © 1927, 1928, 1929, 1930, 1936, 1938, 1940 and 1974 The New Yorker Magazine Inc.

Excerpts from *Shakespeare and Company,* copyright © 1959 by Sylvia Beach and renewed 1987 by Frederic Beach Dennis, reprinted by permission of Harcourt Brace & Company.

Excerpts from *Janet Flanner's World: Uncollected Writings 1932-1975,* copyright © 1979 by Natalia Danesi Murray, reprinted by permission of Harcourt Brace & Company and Martin Secker & Warburg, Ltd.

Library of Congress Cataloging-in-Publication Data is available.

ISBN 978-1-61902-179-2

Cover and interior design by VJB/Scribe

COUNTERPOINT
1919 Fifth Street
Berkeley, CA 94710
www.counterpointpress.com

Printed in the United States of America
Distributed by Publishers Group West

10 9 8 7 6 5 4 3 2 1

To my nieces
Jennifer Levy-Lunt,
une femme de la rive gauche
and Isabella Jane Schiller,
une femme de l'avenir

Contents

Dramatis Personae

BERENICE ABBOTT American photographer, she began her career by taking portraits of her friends in Man Ray's studio during her lunch hour.

MARGARET ANDERSON Founder and editor of *The Little Review*, one of the most important avant-garde literary magazines between the wars.

DJUNA BARNES Novelist, journalist, satirist and visual artist, her best known work is the "underground classic," *Nightwood*.

NATALIE CLIFFORD BARNEY Immensely wealthy, and notoriously lesbian, American writer and salon hostess who lived in Paris for 70 years.

SYLVIA BEACH A Presbyterian minister's daughter, she established the bookshop, Shakespeare and Company, and was the first publisher of James Joyce's *Ulysses*.

GERMAINE BEAUMONT The protégée and intimate friend of Colette, she was a French journalist and novelist who was awarded the prestigious Prix Theophraste Renaudot for literature.

ROMAINE BROOKS American painter of intense portraits in muted colors, she was the lifelong friend of Natalie Barney.

BRYHER (WINIFRED ELLERMAN) English heiress, publisher, writer, patron of the arts, and anti-fascist resistance worker, she was the lifelong friend of poet H.D.

LILY DE CLERMONT-TONNERRE A close friend of Natalie Barney's and Gertrude Stein's, she was a controversial writer of extreme political views, first on the left and in later years on the right.

COLETTE One of France's most highly regarded authors, Colette wrote hundreds of short stories, novels, and essays.

NANCY CUNARD English scion of the Cunard steamship family, she dismissed her parents' upper-class values to become a poet, wide-eyed radical, and founder of the avant-garde Hours Press.

H.D. (HILDA DOOLITTLE) Poet and novelist based primarily in London, with forays into Paris, she was muse to Ezra Pound, analysand of Sigmund Freud, and a proponent of "Imagism."

JANET FLANNER American journalist who commented in *The New Yorker* on life in Paris for 40 years.

GISÈLE FREUND German-Jewish refugee photographer who photographed all the famous and soon-to-be famous writers in France.

EILEEN GRAY Irish designer and architect who evolved her own sparse, elegant Modernist style, and who lived on the Left Bank of Paris for 75 years.

RADCLYFFE HALL English author of the controversial novel *The Well of Loneliness* (1928) which pleaded sympathy for lesbians and was banned in Britain until 1948.

JANE HEAP Co-editor, with Margaret Anderson, of *The Little Review*, and unofficial literary agent for Gertrude Stein.

MARIE LAURENCIN French painter who frequented the salons of Natalie Barney and Gertrude Stein.

GEORGETTE LEBLANC French opera singer who lived for twenty years with editor Margaret Anderson.

MINA LOY English-born Modernist poet and designer, her work was published in many of the small literary magazines.

ADRIENNE MONNIER French writer and editor, she ran the leading bookshop for French avant-garde literature, La Maison des Amis des Livres.

NOEL MURPHY American singer whose home in Orgeval, outside Paris, was a weekend gathering-place for many of the expatriate women.

SOLITA SOLANO Editor, novelist, poet, and journalist, she compromised her own writing career to provide emotional and practical support to Janet Flanner for 50 years.

GERTRUDE STEIN The best known and most prolific of the female Modernist writers in Paris, she was also an art collector and ran a weekly salon.

ALICE B. TOKLAS Lifelong companion, secretary, publisher, and muse to Gertrude Stein.

RENÉE VIVIEN A gifted poet, neighbor of Colette and lover of Natalie Barney, she died in Paris at the age of 31.

DOLLY WILDE An English writer who strongly resembled and admired her uncle Oscar; she abused drugs and alcohol to the point of self-destruction.

THELMA WOOD Silverpoint artist and sculptor, she had a tortured romance with Djuna Barnes in Paris in the twenties.

PREFACE TO THE 2013 EDITION

It seems incredible to me that this book was first published nearly twenty years ago. But on the other hand, so much has happened in the intervening years that twenty can't be nearly enough.

I was living in London in the early 1990s when I became immersed in the research for this book, and had to travel for weeks at a time to the Library of Congress, the Beinecke Rare Book and Manuscript Library at Yale, the Djuna Barnes collection at the University of Maryland, Princeton University Library Department of Rare Books and Special Collections, and other archives holding the letters and photographs of what I had thought of, absurdly and proprietarily, as "my women." There was no way around making a personal visit to each and every collection. So when the Library of Congress denied me access to Janet Flanner and Solita Solano's photographs, on the grounds that they had not been fully inventoried and were not yet open to the public, I simply could not accept that response; without them there would be no book (or film—I was researching the documentary *Paris Was a Woman* at the same time). So I begged and pleaded, and finally agreed or offered, I can't recall which, to meet with an archivist and identify people in the photographs and generally assist with moving the inventory process forward so others could use the collection. After all, by that time the Library of Congress had been holding this gold mine of material for twenty-five years.

I mailed these pleas out by the Royal Mail (this was before it lost its 350-year monopoly) and they were delivered by the United States Postal Service. Email did not yet exist, nor did the World Wide Web. Today it is possible to save on international airfare and hotels and postage stamps and hours of identifying fuzzy, fading snapshots in exchange for access to the collection. Now without even getting out of bed in the morning you can Google the Janet Flanner collection at the Library of Congress, choose the images you like, already clearly identified, and order them online.

As members of my generation have often lamented, something is gained and something is lost in that. I've mentioned the time and money saved, but what is lost is far less quantifiable. I was able to hold the papers of "my women" in my hands, trace their handwriting with my fingertips (covered with white cotton gloves as per archive regulations), find afterthoughts in the margins of letters, often witty or wicked, or added by the recipient when she disagreed with the sender. There were occasionally handwritten captions on the back of snapshots, still today off the radar of the Internet world, such as when Janet Flanner identified a photo of a very old Alice B. Toklas as "the most widowed woman I know." My favorite of all of these findings was buried in a notebook of Gertrude Stein's: in her undisciplined hand scrawl, in faint pencil, I came across the line for which she has become most famous, "Rose is a rose is a rose"—and below that, in far fainter pencil, almost invisible, she added "She is my rose."

The digital revolution is only one aspect of all that has changed. This month, the French Parliament voted to approve gay/lesbian marriage and same-sex adoption, a measure that will put France on the map as one of the foremost countries in the world for LGBT rights. What would the women in this book, almost all of them lesbian, make of this news? It's hard to know, given how completely unimaginable such a development would have been in their lifetimes, but I will venture a guess. They traded the ordinary, expected lives of wife and mother awaiting them in their hometowns for the extraordinary, unexpected lives they could live in Paris. They chose to live outside the social paradigm, and I can imagine that some of them, surely Janet Flanner or Natalie Barney, would reject even these reconfigured roles of wife and mother, however hard won and welcome they may be today. On the other hand, others among them, such as Gertrude Stein or Sylvia Beach, lived in personal relationships that in many ways emulated traditional gender roles—but always with a twist. And I'll speculate farther: had they embraced such social progress in their own time (granted, an anachronistic formulation), and gained full entry into mainstream society, most likely we would not know of them today.

The world has changed and we've changed. I am not sure this is the book the "I" of today would have written, at least written quite this way. History too is a living, breathing, ever-changing thing. Women in this circle that I hadn't discovered back then, such as Nadine Hwang,[1] who lived in Paris in the 1930s and 1940s and had a substantial love affair with Natalie Clifford Barney, have since surfaced, as if they have just walked into the room and become part of the conversation.

Faulkner famously wrote, "The past is not dead, it's not even past." These women, all long dead, continue to be part of the cultural discourse, a discourse that keeps changing. Debates over their legacy still rage, no more so than in the case of Gertrude Stein, who manages, paradoxically, to be one of the best known but least read of all American authors, a woman who seems to arouse love and hate in equal measure. I have to ask myself why she continues to be so threatening to so many.

In the last few years, a new vitriol has been directed at Gertrude Stein. Most previous condemnations of her have been of a literary nature, but this new one is political. I can't help feeling that the choice of Gertrude Stein as the focus of such malice, then and now, is motivated by the same toxic cocktail of homophobia and anti-Semitism and misogyny. She stands accused, by a small but very vocal group of historians, politicians, and pundits, of being a Nazi collaborator —she must have been, or how else did she as a Jewish lesbian survive the Holocaust? Why weren't she and Alice deported from France, or worse? Why would the two women choose to remain friends with Bernard Faÿ, who it turns out *was* a Nazi collaborator? How was it that her "degenerate" art collection was miraculously spared?

The curious thing is that the indictments are not based on information (or misinformation) that has newly come to light; they are merely a new spin on old stories, a spin that has taken on the force of a twister. Gertrude Stein's playfulness with language and well-known wit have been contorted against her, so that a facetious, anti-Hitler comment she made in *The New York Times* in 1934 ("I say that Hitler ought to have the peace prize ... because he is removing all elements of contest and struggle from Germany") becomes, in the humorless minds of the misguided moral police, a "fact" that Gertrude Stein actually endorsed Hitler for the Nobel Prize rather than a jibe against him. Not many people, certainly not enough, in *The New York Times* or elsewhere, were speaking out against Hitler as early as 1934, but all of us today with 20/20 hindsight would certainly have been among the few visionaries. Under a headline printed in August of that year, "Hitler Endorsed by 9 to 1 in Poll on his Dictatorship ..." *The New York Times* informs us "it is not yet a matter for international concern." (*NY Times*, August 20, 1934.)

While there are Stein detractors popping up around every corner,

ABOVE: Gertrude Stein with the young sculptor and silverpoint artist Thelma Wood: their contrasting appearances reveal some of the disparity in age, sexuality, and economic class among the women in Paris.

Gertrude continues to have her defenders as well.[2] Some of them came together to refute each thin accusation upon which this house of cards is built. As the poet and literary scholar Charles Bernstein points out in *Gertrude Stein's War Years: Setting the Record Straight*, "This willful, multiply repeated, misrepresentation of Stein's remark in a 1934 *New York Times* interview is a little like saying that Mel Brooks includes a tribute to Hitler in *The Producers*."[3]

When this recent brouhaha erupted, I turned to the pages in this book about Gertrude Stein's life during World War II. I wondered if there was something I would want to revise in light of these developments, if I had disregarded important information out of sheer stubbornness or overidentification with my subject. I see that I allude to but do not address in depth some of the obvious contradictions inherent in Gertrude Stein's character. I could have written more on that subject, had I known she would be under such attack. I suppose it is to be expected that when you return to something you wrote so many years ago there would be an urge to revise it, but I resist the temptation; I stand by what I wrote back then, and not just about Gertrude Stein but about all of these women, throughout the book.

It has been a heartache to me that *Paris Was a Woman* has been out of print for so many years. Thus I am enormously grateful to editorial director Jack Shoemaker and production manager Emma Cofod of Counterpoint Press for ushering it back into print. May new generations find sustenance and inspiration from the women in these pages, and create their own legacies.

ABOVE: "Quite unexpectedly suddenly my name has become very well known in America and publishers over there are eager ..."

PREFACE TO THE 1995 EDITION

O ften films start out as books, but in my case this book grew out of a film project. My partner Greta Schiller and I felt that time was overdue for a comprehensive documentary film on the women of the Left Bank. We began the enormous research and fund-raising work, never dreaming that four years would pass before we saw its completion.

I have had many wonderful experiences in the process. Visiting the Fonds Littéraire Jacques Doucet in Paris, for instance, Greta and I were taken into a small closet off the main reading room. We wondered what on earth would be revealed by the head archivist, François Chapon; he had already shown us Natalie Barney's furniture, paintings, and chest of private love letters. We were completely surprised by what came next—François Chapon, who had known Natalie Barney when he was a young man, opened a beautiful inlay box to reveal a plait of her hair.

From Paris Greta and I hired a car and drove down to Bilignin, the village in the Rhône region where Gertrude and Alice had their country home. Using *The Alice B. Toklas Cookbook* as our travel guide, we stopped in some of the best hidden-away country restaurants in all of France. We laughed about how fortunate we were that this trip ostensibly was our 'work.' We loved coming upon, at long last, the signs indicating Bilignin, placed on each end of a little country lane. Between the two village signs were fewer than a dozen farmhouses, many cows, a beautiful double row of old, sturdy oak trees and a big gate—behind which stood Gertrude and Alice's big grey house. We could have been in the 1930s when Gertrude and Alice lived there; we almost could have been in the 1830s as well, for how little the village has changed.

I want to thank the many people who made possible my research for both the film and book: at the Library of Congress, Beverly Brannon in the prints and photographs division and Fred Bauman in the manuscripts division. At the Fonds Littéraire Jacques Doucet, Nicole Prevot and François Chapon. At the Sylvia Beach collection at Princeton University, Margaret Sherry. For assistance with the letters, manuscripts and photographs of Djuna Barnes, Ruth M. Alvarez at the McKeldin Library, University of Maryland at College Park, and L. Rebecca Johnson Melvin at the University of Delaware Library. At Yale University, Beinecke Rare Book and Manuscript Library, Patricia Willis and Daniele McClellan.

Most of my research took place in these archives, where I sifted through letters, photographs, and other worn, fragile materials, feeling inspired and transported by them into the past. Nonetheless, I also read numerous contemporary books on the subject and I am deeply indebted to the scholars and biographers who paved the way for me and brought attention to these women's lives and work, including Shari Benstock, Noel Riley Fitch, Catharine R. Stimpson, Meryl Secrest, Brenda Wineapple, and in particular, Karla Jay, who supported this project all along the way.

Frances Berrigan, executive producer, and Greta Schiller, director, of the documentary film have been the best possible colleagues on this project, and I look forward to many more collaborations with them both. My agent, Faith Evans, immediately saw exciting possibilities in what was, back then, just a vague idea—which it may well have stayed had it not been for her enthusiasm and consistent encouragement. My editor Sara Dunn firmly believed in the project throughout (even though she kept trying to restrain my growing selection of photographs) and gave me invaluable guidance. I want to thank as well all the others at Pandora who skillfully transformed the manuscript into a book, including Belinda Budge, Miranda Wilson, Michele Turney, designers Jo Ridgeway and Jerry Goldie and my copy editor Ruth Petrie. Elizabeth Wilson kindly read the book in manuscript form; her comments, always so intelligent, are greatly appreciated. Thanks also to Marina Ganzerli, Miles McKane, Kirsten Lenk, and Florence Fradelizi for their assistance with the research in crucial moments. For help in tracking down obscure references and images and juggling all sorts of details, my endless thanks to Melissa Cahill Tonelli.

The photographer Gisèle Freund, who agreed to be interviewed for the film, subsequently spent many enlightening hours with us on various trips to Paris. For her inspired conversation, carried on in a baffling mixture of French, German, and English, (she speaks four languages, but, according to her, none of them well) she has my total admiration. Many thanks to Berthe Cleyrergue and the late Sam

Steward for also agreeing to be interviewed and offering their precious firsthand memories.

Mark Finch was always an interested, sympathetic listener to my ideas and frustrations throughout the writing of both this and my previous book. I wish it were possible to thank him for his unflagging confidence in me, and for his countless acts of genuine friendship over the past decade.

Introduction

Paris Was a Woman

Renée Vivien dreamt of Paris, "that loved and longed-for city"; for Colette it was the "City of Love." Janet Flanner believed that the Seine gave Paris a special anatomy that made her "one of the loveliest cities left on earth." It was the Left Bank of the Seine which first called out to Adrienne Monnier, and years later continued "to call me and to keep me." Sylvia Beach stated, with typical modesty and understatement, that she was "extremely fond of Paris, I must confess." Djuna Barnes would cry out, more passionately, "there's a longing in me to be in Paris."

Women with creative energy and varying degrees of talent, women with a passion for art and literature, women without the obligations that come with husbands and children, were especially drawn to the Left Bank, and never with more urgency and excitement than in the first quarter of this century. It was not simply its beauty but that rare promise of freedom that drew these women to it. They came from as near as Savoy and Burgundy and from as far as London, Berlin, and New York, Chicago, Indiana, and California—before the days of the airplane. They came for their own individual, private reasons, some of which they themselves perhaps never fully fathomed. But they also came because Paris offered them, as women, a unique and extraordinary world.

LEFT: Adrienne Monnier entering her bookshop, the birthplace of several Modernist literary movements.

Individual biographies of many of these women have been published in the past decade, and Shari Benstock's impeccable resource, *Women of the Left Bank,* serves as both thoughtful literary analysis and detailed group biography of the female Modernists. Conferences have been held on the writings of Djuna Barnes, and newly edited and restored manuscripts of Gertrude Stein have been published. Women artists, writers, scholars, publishers, and many others continue to be inspired and fascinated by the women of the Left Bank, and the stories of their lives and works are no longer restricted to academic circles.

This growing body of work on the Paris of the 1920s and 30s calls into question the myths and clichés which have become enshrined in the popular imagination, fuelled by the many accounts of American male expatriates such as Robert McAlmon's *Being Geniuses Together** and Samuel Putnam's *Paris Was Our Mistress,* which emphasize the bars and brothels inhabited by the macho, hard-drinking artists. Their nameless, ever-patient wives barely got a look-in. More recently, Humphrey Carpenter embellishes these myths in his *Geniuses Together,* a boastful chronicle of boozing, gambling, and sexual exploits. We learn that Hemingway was recklessly gambling away his wife Hadley's money at the Paris racetracks while James Joyce and Robert McAlmon were slogging their way through an entire menu of French drinks. Malcolm Cowley, who later wrote *Exile's Return: A Literary Odyssey of the 1920s,* got into a violent bar brawl with the proprietor of the Rotonde and so earned himself admission into the inner sanctum of the male expatriate community.

The twin emphases on drinking and sexual exploits dominate the image we now have of Paris in the twenties. Yet the women's experiences of both of these "freedoms" were very different. Sylvia Beach was a teetotaler, and although it was she who introduced the legendary writers James Joyce and Valéry Larbaud to each other, she did not join them when they met, regularly, "in that American bar in the Latin Quarter, whither his friend James Joyce calls him whenever he wants to read a new work to [Larbaud]."[1] Natalie Barney claimed that "being born intoxicated, I drink only water," although she was occasionally seen taking a few sips of an excellent French wine. Gertrude Stein and Alice Toklas, it is well known, had no tolerance for drunks; they were not invited a second time. The English writer and publisher, Winifred Ellerman, who called herself Bryher, preferred water to wine and soon after arriving in Paris decided to refuse all alcohol since "drinks and *la poésie pure* did not mix." She looked at the drunken faces of a group of male Modernists and, "Suddenly I realized to my horror that it was a vicarage garden party in reverse. These rebels were no more free from the conventions that they fastened upon themselves than a group of old ladies gossiping over their knitting."[2]

Janet Flanner, who loved nothing more than a good gossip, washed down with an aperitif of cinzano and fruit juice at the Café des Deux Magots, would probably not have agreed, and neither would Nancy Cunard or Djuna Barnes, who often joined her there. Yet all three were hardworking writers drawn to Paris for the freedom it offered women—the freedom to work. When we look at the cumulative accomplishment of these authors, poets, painters, book publishers, photographers, "little magazine" editors, and booksellers, it becomes clear that the continually fostered myth of lazy afternoons in cafés and wild nights in Montparnasse bars simply does not fit.

"Sexual freedom" was also a part of the mythology—and also, something most of the Modernist women could do without. According to Djuna Barnes's biographer, Andrew Field, women did want this freedom, but simply weren't able to handle it: "… sexual freedom came too suddenly, and [they were] ill-prepared to cope with the freedom of Paris. The stage set was magnificent, but most could not master their parts."[3]

He assumes that so-called sexual freedom was indeed a goal for women, or that it meant the same thing to women as to men. But did the model of sexual freedom for men—sex without commitment, or with many partners instead of one—comprise freedom for women? For whom was the stage set magnificent; for whom was it designed?

When Robert McAlmon tried to kiss Adrienne Monnier in a taxi he received not a polite rebuke but a heavy bite on his lip. Ezra Pound tried a similar move on Bryher, with equally unsuccessful results. These were but two of many women on the Left Bank for whom sexual freedom did not mean being readily available to men, but rather freedom from the heterosexual imperative. It meant freedom to love as they chose—in their case, other women.

There were, inevitably, unpleasant literary consequences for women who rejected individual men or men in general. Ezra Pound felt Djuna Barnes's literary reputation was overrated and "in need of deflating."

Men labeled Nancy Cunard a nymphomaniac and therefore fair game, so when Richard Aldington walked in and, in her words, "pounced," she paid a high price for refusing his "favors." Aldington viciously attacked her as being a predatory, ruthless destroyer of men in his short story "Now Lies She There." William Carlos Williams, a man who had been shocked by the presence of lesbians at Natalie Barney's salon, wrote publicly about Adrienne and Bryher in such unwarranted terms of disgust that Bryher was driven to seek legal recourse.

When we pay attention to these women's stories, we find a different image of Paris emerging, which is not that of one long party lasting the entire decade of the twenties. Even the unrelenting cultural fascination with "the twenties" ignores the reality that many of the expatriate women arrived in Paris much earlier (Natalie Barney and Eileen Gray, for instance, came in 1902; Gertrude Stein in 1903), and stayed much later. Most made Paris their permanent home, surviving one or even two world wars.

How did this city appear to them upon their arrival? They became enchanted by the busy outdoor market at Les Halles on the Right Bank, the romantic bookstalls and fishermen along the Seine, the outdoor café by the lake in the Bois de Boulogne where ladies of leisure met for lunch. They walked by children playing with wooden sailboats in the fountain in the Luxembourg Gardens. The sounds they heard most often were of church bells and of horses' hooves on cobblestone passageways. They settled on the Left Bank, close to the river, and began to work. There they created three milieux which were to change the cultural landscape of Paris: Sylvia Beach's and Adrienne Monnier's bookshops in the rue de l'Odeon, and Natalie Barney's and Gertrude Stein's salons in the rue Jacob and rue de Fleurus, respectively.

It was not that Paris was culturally more "liberated" than England or America in its attitudes towards women, but simply that it left its foreigners alone. Asked why she liked to live among the French, Gertrude Stein wrote, "Well the reason is very simple their life belongs to them so your life can belong to you ..."[4]

If the goal was to have their lives belonging to themselves, it was no coincidence that virtually all the women writers and artists in Paris had neither husbands nor children. (Some of the women who found themselves pregnant, such as Janet Flanner and Djuna Barnes, had miscarriages or abortions or, in the case of Romaine Brooks, gave the child up for adoption. The few with children—H.D. and Colette each had a daughter—were not regularly based in Paris and also had other people to care for the children.) Of those who had married at some point, all were divorced or widowed. Katherine Anne Porter, an American expatriate writer in France who *was* married, betrayed feelings of jealousy towards Gertrude Stein for being able to have her own life. After Gertrude's death, she wrote about her in *Harper's Magazine*, situating her in

> the company of Amazons which nineteenth-century America produced among its many prodigies: not-men, not-women, answerable to no function in either sex, whose careers were carried on, and how successfully, in whatever field they chose … who lived in public and by the public and played out their self-assumed, self-created roles in such masterly freedom as only a few early medieval queens had equaled. Freedom to them meant precisely freedom from men and their stuffy rules for women. They usurped with a high hand the traditional masculine privileges of movement, choice, and the use of direct, personal power …[5]

This "company of Amazons" was a self-consciously created community whose lives intertwined in multiple, often surprising ways. Yet they were not a monolithic group; divisions and conflicts existed along lines of nationality, economic class, talent, artistic priorities, political perspective, and sexuality. Gertrude Stein's and H.D.'s writing had nothing in common, yet friendship and respect for each other's work overrode literary differences.

Their financial situations were as varied as their artistic goals. Some were heiresses, as Natalie Barney, Romaine Brooks, and Bryher were, while some like Djuna Barnes lived on the *largesse* of others. Others, such as Alice B. Toklas, lived on small family allowances. Janet Flanner was the only one with a regular paycheck; Berenice Abbott recalled that Janet always could afford to dress elegantly as a result.

Many of the women were lesbian or bisexual; all felt a primary emotional, if not sexual, attachment to other women. Yet there were many ways of defining (or not defining) their romantic attachments: Gertrude Stein wrote about her "wife," Janet Flanner talked of her "emotional friendships," and Sylvia Beach was silent on the subject. Their intimate relationships also arranged themselves in a variety of constellations that, in forging new territory, followed no set pattern or predetermined rules.

Although the women were of different nationalities and religions, they were all white, despite there being many influential Black American women living in Paris at that time—who were attracted to Paris precisely because they found no "color bar" there. Author and editor Jessie Redmon Fauset had found that in Paris "nobody cares—not even Americans, it seems—whether an artist is white, black or yellow or, as Forster says in *A Passage to India*, 'pink-gray.'"[6] She met more writers and artists in four months in Paris than she had in four years in New York. But in general the encounters between black and white women did not lead to enduring friendships.

Among the outstanding black women entertainers who made Paris their home were Josephine Baker, Bricktop, Adelaide Hall, Florence Mills, and Mabel Mercer, while Elizabeth Welch was a frequent visitor from England. Florence Mills and Adelaide Hall were stars of The Blackbirds, an all-black show of over 100 performers that played at the Moulin Rouge. Originally brought over for the tourists and expatriates, the troupe found its best audience among the enthusiastic French. Of all the Black Americans performing on the Parisian stage, Josephine Baker was indisputably the most celebrated. She arrived in 1925 at the age of 18, as part of a chorus line with the first Black American stage company ever to tour Europe. Just off the ship and on the train to Paris, she fell immediately in love with France—but that was nothing compared with the way France would soon fall in love with her.

Bricktop was born Ada Smith in Chicago, and ran a popular club across town in Montmartre, where she sang Cole Porter songs like an angel and knew all her customers by name. Although English painter Nina Hamnett, American writer Kay Boyle, and the famous Montparnasse model Kiki were all seen on occasion in Bricktop's, she was better friends with her "regulars"—among them Robert McAlmon (whom she called "the big spendin' man") and Man Ray, who could always be found at the bar.

There were few social connections between the black entertainers and the white literary women. Janet Flanner and Adrienne Monnier both wrote enthusiastically about Josephine Baker's performance,

ABOVE: The singer and nightclub owner Ada Smith, nicknamed "Bricktop" because of her red hair.

but neither mentions meeting her, despite Colette being their mutual friend. During the twenties, Colette was one of Josephine Baker's closest friends, their intimacy based in part on a shared love of animals.

While black entertainers were dazzling Paris with their Afro-American rhythms and styles, other, mostly European, women were flocking to Paris and shaking up its cultural life on other fronts. Architecture, photography, painting, ballet, theater and costume design, and filmmaking were just some of the visual and performing arts of the 1920s in which women pioneered and flourished. From Russia, the avant-garde painters and theatre designers Alexandra Exter and Natalya Goncharova came to Paris where Cubist, Futurist, and Constructivist influences were discernible in their colorful, rhythmically active compositions. From England, Modernist designer and architect Eileen Gray came to Paris to discover Cubism and art deco and to enjoy the companionship of other female visual artists, including Romaine Brooks and Berenice Abbott. From Germany, photographers Marianne Breslauer and Germaine Krull arrived and used the city itself as their model for Modernist compositions in black and white. From France, Germaine Dulac was an innovator of avant-garde

filmmaking, often with a focus on women's themes. Most of these visual artists crossed paths with the literary women and the confluence of such creativity had cultural implications for them all. The cast of characters was not limited to either women or foreigners, but the *mise-en-scène* of pre-war Paris was both international and female.

Paris has often been imagined as a mysterious, seductive woman, both mistress and muse to generations of male poets. Women drawn to the allure of Paris were also responding to the female qualities of a city which allowed them to express themselves in less conventional, more substantive ways than simply as romanticized mistress or muse. Whatever perspectives, needs, or backgrounds the women of the Left Bank seem to have in common, it was the intangible but irresistible promise of Paris that united them. Gertrude Stein wrote in 1939 that, "The only personality I would like to write about … is Paris, France, that is where we all were, and it was natural for us to be there."[7] As they searched to find and create the conditions by which they could love and work and live, they transformed the character of the city itself. For them, Paris was neither a fantasized young *cocotte,* clichéd old mistress, nor the idealized muse of the male poet's imagination. For nearly half a century, she became a fascinating, creative, intelligent woman.

*Robert McAlmon wrote *Being Geniuses Together: 1920–1930* in 1938. It was revised, with additional material by Kay Boyle, in 1968.

LEFT: Sylvia Beach, young and determined

ADRIENNE ▪ ▪ MONNIER

1

ODÉONIA:
THE COUNTRY OF BOOKS

Twenty-three-year-old Adrienne Monnier realized a childhood dream in November 1915 when she opened a small bookshop on the rue de l'Odéon in the sixth arrondissement. Its location in the heart of the artistic and intellectual center of Paris was no accident:

> The Left Bank called me and even now it does not
> cease to call me and to keep me. I cannot imagine
> that I could ever leave it, any more than an organ
> can leave the place that is assigned to it in the body.[1]

She loved books passionately and read each one before bringing it into her shop. What we perceive as an "ordinary" and practical business (although at the time, hardly ordinary for women) she managed to turn into an intellectual and artistic profession. Her bookshop soon became the hub of French avant-garde literature, the birthplace for more than one Modernist movement, and a spontaneous literary salon for many famous and soon-to-be famous writers, including André Breton, Paul Valéry, Colette, Guillaume Apollinaire, Jules Romains, Jean Cocteau, Léon-Paul Fargue and André Gide. Almost four years after Adrienne had opened her bookshop, the young American Sylvia Beach established her own English language bookshop, Shakespeare and Company. Alice B. Toklas later

LEFT: A portrait of Adrienne Monnier in her favorite setting — surrounded by books. Painted by her brother-in-law, Paul Emile Bécat.

recalled that within just a few months, Sylvia had become a "literary personality." Janet Flanner describes the two booksellers:

> The immediate compatibility of these two extraordinary women—Mlle Monnier, buxom as an abbess, placidly picturesque in the costume she had permanently adopted, consisting of a long, full gray skirt, a bright velveteen waistcoat, and a white blouse, and slim, jacketed Sylvia, with her schoolgirl white collar and big colored bowknot, in the style of Colette's *Claudine à l'école*—eventually had an important canalizing influence on French-American literary relations as they flowed, almost like a new major cultural traffic, up and down the Rue de l'Odéon.[2]

An American minister's daughter from Princeton, New Jersey, Sylvia Beach had come to Paris at the age of 29 because of a professed love for France and for contemporary French literature. It was 1917, four years into the worst war in history, and before long she left Paris to enlist in the war effort. It would be two years before she returned, bringing an engraved cigarette lighter as a gift for Adrienne Monnier, whom she had met shortly after her arrival in France. Sylvia Beach's biographer, Noel Riley Fitch, describes that initial meeting:

> The story began in Paris on a cold, gusty March afternoon in 1917. A shy young woman named Sylvia Beach hesitated at the door of a Left Bank bookshop and lending library, La Maison des Amis des Livres. The owner, a self-assured young French writer and publisher named Adrienne Monnier, got up quickly from her desk and drew her visitor into the shop, greeting her warmly. The two talked the afternoon away, each declaring love for the language and literature of the other.[3]

ABOVE: Sylvia worked as a volunteer farmhand in Touraine, as all the men had left for the front. She then volunteered for the Red Cross in Serbia at the war's end.

The developing relationship between Sylvia and Adrienne was crucial to the flowering of English and American literature in France. It was the example and inspiration of Adrienne Monnier that guided Sylvia towards her life's calling in the service of literature. From the practical perspective, Adrienne was the one who took on the logistical problems of setting up Shakespeare and Company, obtaining the necessary business permit and negotiating with the concierge of the former laundry. Sylvia recalled that when they first went to view the premises, Adrienne

> point[ed] to the words "gros" and "fin" on either side of the door, meaning they did both sheets and fine linen. Adrienne, who was rather plump, placed herself under the "gros" and told me to stand under the "fin." "That's you and me," she said.[4]

This sense of humor was key to their relationship, perhaps even more important than their shared love of French literature. Adrienne wrote:

> This young American displayed an original and most attaching personality. She spoke French fluently with … an energetic and incisive way of pronouncing words … In her conversation there were neither hesitations nor pauses; words never failed her; on occasion she deliberately invented them, she proceeded then by an adaption of English, by a mixture or extension of French vocables, all that with the exquisite sense of our language. Her finds were generally so happy, so charmingly funny, that they at once came into usage—our usage—as if they had always existed; one could not keep from repeating them, and one tried to imitate them. To sum it up, this young American had a great deal of humor, let us say more: she was humor itself.[5]

Their devotion to each other lasted until Adrienne's death in 1955, when Katherine Anne Porter wrote to Sylvia: "Adrienne—you and Adrienne, for I thought of you together, even though you were both so distinct as individuals and friends in my mind …"[6]

Ostensibly in the same profession, Adrienne's focus was books and words while Sylvia's was readers and writers. Perhaps it was these different emphases that softened any potential competition between the

ABOVE: The two young women who found themselves at the center of French-American literary relations.

two establishments, so much so that Sylvia "always consulted [Adrienne] before taking an important step. She was such a wise counselor, and she was, besides, a sort of partner in the firm."[7]

Educated in Latin and French, philosophy, mathematics, and history, Adrienne had a love of words and books not limited to those written by others; she published a volume of poetry in 1923, called *La Figure,* and a collection of prose in 1932. In addition to her bookshop work she managed to contribute articles to numerous journals including *Commerce* and *Mesures* (for both of which she was the administrator for a short while), *Nouvelle Revue Française, Figaro Littéraire,* and *Les Lettres Nouvelles.* Widely accepted as a leading authority on French avant-garde literature, she received letters from around the world. The great Russian film director, Sergei Eisenstein, requested that she "writ[e] me a line or two about what is the great *'épatage'* of to-day in French literature!"[8]

Sylvia, by contrast, had no formal education and did not write anything but her highly guarded memoirs late in life, and a translation of *Barbarian in Asia* by Henri Michaux. To Bryher she confessed that "… I only wish I had exercised with the pen a little all these years, and now knew how to write, as Gertrude would call it, but I didn't and don't."[9] In a letter to the editor of her memoirs, she turned her inhibitions about writing into a joke:

> About my education, the less said the better. I ain't had none: never went to school and wouldn't have learned anything if I had went. You will have to copy what goes for T.S. Eliot: say I have degrees from all those places, same as him.[10]

Janet Flanner, with that acerbic tongue she was known for in her political journalism, claimed that

> Sylvia herself did not have a literary mind or much literary taste though in time a certain sense of literature rubbed off into her from the people around her. What she instinctively recognized and was attracted to was merely literary genius or flashes and fractions of it, or of tremendous great talent …[11]

This talent preferably came in the form of a writer. Even more than books, it was the writers that she loved most and made her life's work, evidenced by the shop's interior in which more wall space was devoted to portraits of writers than to books. Man Ray and Berenice Abbott were "the official portraitists of 'the Crowd,'" as Sylvia Beach dubbed them, until Gisèle Freund came through Paris in the mid-thirties and made a career of photographing all the great writers and thinkers on the Left Bank.

In 1919, Sylvia was in the process of choosing a path for her own

ABOVE: According to Janet Flanner, this check represented Sylvia's mother's life savings, which she sent so that Sylvia could open her bookshop.

Adrienne and Sylvia during a Sunday outing to Rocfoin, where Adrienne's family lived. Occasionally James Joyce (seated, left) would join them.

career that would not seem "useless" in comparison to her war efforts. She responded to her mother's futile pleas to return to Princeton by sending a telegram: "Opening bookshop in Paris. Please send money." Not wealthy herself, her mother obliged with $3,000. Sylvia was able to open the shop.

Like Sylvia, Adrienne had no brothers and therefore was the recipient of some family money. Her father, a postal clerk who worked on the trains, received compensation for near fatal injuries in a railroad accident, the only money her family ever had. Adrienne, a staunch pacifist, believed herself "blessed by the Goddess of War": in addition to the compensation money, the recruitment of men into the First World War created unprecedented professional opportunities for women such as herself. Adrienne always found these two factors that enabled her to open her shop—world war and family tragedy—ironic and bittersweet.

After the initial start-up funds, Sylvia continued to receive occasional financial assistance from her mother, who often sold her jewelry for this purpose. Adrienne's family sent both Adrienne and Sylvia fresh vegetables from their home in Rocfoin, a small town southwest of Paris, where for many years the two women spent their Sundays. These contributions supplemented the meager earnings of the two bookshops.

Sylvia described her first meeting with the people who would become two of her most regular book-borrowers in the shop's early days:

> Not long after I had opened my bookshop, two women came
> … One of them, with a very fine face, was stout, wore a long
> robe, and, on her head, a most becoming top of a basket. She
> was accompanied by a slim, dark whimsical woman: she
> reminded me of a gypsy.[12]

They were, of course, Gertrude Stein and Alice B. Toklas. Gertrude set out to help the shop by circulating an advertisement for it:

> Not a country not a door send them away to sit on the floor.
> Cakes. This is not the world. Can you remember.

Alice and Janet Flanner both claimed this succeeded in drawing in new customers.

3 avril 1920

Chère Mademoiselle,

Je vous rappelle que c'est mercredi 7
que nous fêtons chez moi : 18 rue
de l'Odéon (5 h.)

En attendant le grand plaisir de
vous voir, je vous envoie, ainsi
qu'à votre amie, l'assurance de
ma vive sympathie.

Adrienne Monnier

From the start, Sylvia and Adrienne were much more than booksellers. Adrienne, in particular, was determined to alter people's, and especially women's, reading habits and relation to books. In her essay "Les Amies des Livres," she offered a feminist analysis of women's relationship to books, and catered to that relationship in the way she ran her bookshop: she sold inexpensive volumes for curious readers rather than first editions for scholars and collectors, and allowed customers to take books home for a time before deciding whether to buy them. Her free lending library was the first ever in France. Sylvia and Adrienne saw themselves as not only sellers and lenders but also readers and lovers of books, charged with the mission of imparting this love to their customers. Bryher wrote that Sylvia was known for "finding by some intuitive process that she and Adrienne Monnier alone seemed to me to possess, the exact book that an enquirer needed for his development at that particular moment."[13]

In 1921 Shakespeare and Company moved around the corner so that it was almost directly opposite Adrienne's bookshop, and Sylvia moved into Adrienne's apartment a few doors away. After that, Bryher felt that

there was only one street in Paris for me, the rue de l'Odéon. It is association, I suppose, but I have always considered it one of the most beautiful streets in the world. It meant naturally Sylvia and Adrienne and the happy hours that I spent in their libraries.[14]

Bryher and Sylvia became friends soon after the shop opened, and they remained close for the rest of their lives. After more than thirty years of friendship, Sylvia wrote,

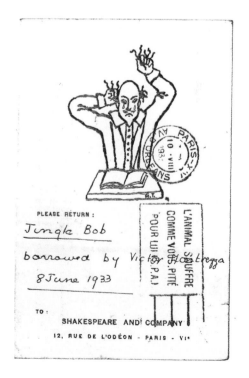

LEFT: Adrienne formally invited Gertrude and Alice to her house, soon after they had joined Sylvia's lending library.

RIGHT: Shakespeare pulled out his hair whenever books were overdue in the lending library.

9

It was in one of the earliest days of "Shakespeare and Company" that you came into my bookshop and my life, dear Bryher, and that we became a Protectorate of yours. We might have had the words: "By Special Appointment to Bryher" painted above the door.[15]

The sister bookshops on the rue de l'Odéon soon became a cultural center of Europe, serving as a gathering place where writers from all over the world met, collected their post and read the latest in the proliferation of literary magazines. The French poet Jules Romains introduced poetry readings at La Maison des Amis des Livres shortly after he met Adrienne in 1917. She had lured him into the bookshop by writing, "At 7 rue de l'Odéon there is a bookseller who loves your work." Soon after, he came by and inquired after Monsieur Monnier. She was thrilled that he hadn't guessed her gender, perhaps suspecting that he would not have taken her seriously enough to come at all. She need not have worried:

I saw in front of me a girl with a round, rosy face, with blue eyes, with blond hair, who, it appeared almost at once, had just entered the service of literature as others decide to enter the service of religion … Already her voice was authoritative and charming; very watched over, very limpid, at once full of music and assurance.[16]

Although poetry readings predominated, occasionally other, non-literary events were held as well, such as a tea in honor of Paul Robeson at Shakespeare and Company, at which he sang Negro Spirituals, thus performing the opening concert of his European tour. The first exhibition of photographs by Gisèle Freund was held in La Maison des Amis des Livres.

In the mid-thirties, Gisèle Freund left Germany at a day's notice with a suitcase containing her unfinished doctoral dissertation, a change of clothing, and a few Deutschmarks. She had been alerted that the police were looking for members of her student group, involved in resistance activities in Frankfurt. Grateful to be safe from the Nazis, she arrived in Paris, not knowing she was the only one of her group to

LEFT: The English writer and publisher Bryher, who used her family wealth to support Shakespeare and Company during its many financial crises.

11

survive. She resumed her studies at the Sorbonne and one day, while browsing through the outdoor stalls on the rue de l'Odéon, selected a book by Jules Romains to buy for two francs. As she opened the shop door of La Maison des Amis des Livres, she met the woman, twenty years her senior, who would become the most influential person in her life. The two women became fast friends, and on busy days Gisèle would help Adrienne in her shop.

Meanwhile Gisèle began taking photographs, using free stock from the front and tail ends of moving picture film. She asked filmmaker friends Bunuel, Dali, and Cocteau to give her these otherwise unusable "short ends," thus enabling her to get started in 35mm still photography. One day she suggested to Adrienne:

> I have an idea, I have a new film in color, I would love to photograph all your friends in color. And she said "that's a wonderful idea," she was always open for new ideas you see, and therefore in less than a year I made all these photographs which now are worldwide known. Not everybody knows who did them, but the photographs are known.[17]

Adrienne decided to hold an exhibition of the photographs in her shop. She rented fifty chairs, hung a white sheet on the wall, and invited the leading authors of Paris to watch their own images projected on the wall. She even reviewed the exhibition in her bookshop magazine:

> I have come back from a voyage to the country of faces. A long voyage undertaken in the company of Gisèle Freund. It was she who was the pilot, she who held the rudder, she who operated the machine for exploring faces. This machine was an ordinary camera loaded with film sensitive to colors … Yes, my voyage with Gisèle Freund has been a great adventure. All the more so because she is a bold photographer and conceals nothing, not she … Thanks to her, we are rich in excellent pictures of most of our best writers. It should be said that her way of projecting the photos on a screen gives very surprising results. Here light plays the role of a sculptor … [18]

And Simone de Beauvoir recalled:

ABOVE: From the balcony of Gisèle Freund's hotel room Adrienne Monnier looks out over her beloved Left Bank.

The place was crowded with famous writers. I don't remember who was there; what has stayed eternally in my mind, however, is the sight of the chairs lined up in rows, the screen glowing in the darkness, and the familiar faces bathed in beautiful color … All the consecrated authors as well as the new talents with a still-uncertain future drifted across the screen before our eyes.[19]

Sylvia and Adrienne were cultural diplomats and ambassadors, introducing writers and artists to each other and delicately balancing artistic temperaments. In the early 1920s, Sylvia Beach introduced Gertrude Stein to French writers such as Valéry Larbaud, the bookshop's official "godfather," whom Gertrude subsequently invited to her salon. In the mid-thirties Sylvia and Adrienne held a large reception in honor of the editors and contributors to *Life and Letters Today,* which Sylvia insisted be a cross-cultural affair. She wrote to Bryher, "I think it is very important for you all to be present, on account of the friendly relations with French writers. And you know it won't be at all formal, never is in our house, and people don't dress up here …"[20] Sylvia also played the role of "tour guide" for young American writers hoping to meet Gertrude Stein:

> Gertrude Stein's admirers, until they had met her and discovered how affable she was, were often "skeered" to approach her without proper protection. So the poor things would come to me, exactly as if I were a guide from one of the tourist agencies, and beg me to take them to see Gertrude Stein.
>
> My tours, arranged with Gertrude and Alice beforehand, took place in the evenings. They were cheerfully endured by the ladies in the pavilion, who were always cordial and hospitable.[21]

Bryher, in her memoirs, wrote that Sylvia "was the perfect Ambassador and I doubt if a citizen has ever done more to spread knowledge of America abroad … Great and humble she mixed us all together …, the bond between us being that we were artists and discoverers."[22]

One young American that she took under her wing was an unknown journalist and "wannabe" writer named Ernest Hemingway. He spent hours in the shop, reading and occasionally buying the many experimental "little magazines" on sale while Sylvia and her assistants babysat his son Bumby. Sylvia found that Hemingway had "the true writer's temperament" which she admired from the start. Adrienne quietly predicted that of all the unknown expatriates adrift in Paris

LEFT: Ernest Hemingway claimed he could write letters but not mail them. As he was in the shop virtually every morning, he probably hand-delivered this letter to Sylvia.

ABOVE: The cultural ambassador in front of her embassy.

ABOVE: Sylvia, Adrienne, and *Ulysses,* disguised as *Shakespeare's Works in One Volume.*

trying to write, Hemingway would be the one to succeed. But Sylvia placed her bet on someone else.

In 1920 Sylvia met James Joyce at a dinner party at the home of French poet André Spire, to which she had been brought by Adrienne and he by Ezra Pound. She recognized him as the author of *A Portrait of the Artist as a Young Man*, although how she came upon this book she couldn't recall: "I don't know. You can never tell how a book-worm gets hold of a book. They simply make for this diet of theirs."[23] She approached him, trembling, and asked, "Is this the great James Joyce?" to which he quietly replied, "James Joyce," and she shook what she described as his "limp, boneless" hand.

Her passionate belief in Joyce's genius led Sylvia into a tremendously risky and courageous undertaking: the publication of *Ulysses*, in 1922, when no established publisher would touch it. Sylvia attempted it because she was, in the words of Janet Flanner, "the intrepid, unselfish, totally inexperienced, and little-moneyed young-lady publisher."[24] Three similarly intrepid, unselfish, and inexperienced women had tried unsuccessfully before her. When Harriet Weaver started the Egoist Press in London specifically for this purpose, the British printers refused to set the type. Margaret Anderson and Jane Heap began publishing *Ulysses* piecemeal in their *Little Review*, then still based in New York, only to have three issues seized by the United States Post Office and a fourth land them in court on an obscenity charge. It managed to become a book only because the French printers in Dijon did not understand English. Even by its eighth edition Sylvia's shop was selling it, at purchasers' request, in false dust covers because of the lingering controversy surrounding it; one cover gave it the title "Shakespeare's Works in One Volume," another "Merry Tales for Little Folks."

Beach served as the "midwife" to Joyce's career, devoting herself to publishing and promoting his work and ensuring that Joyce and his family of four had adequate funds. This twelve-year involvement was not only an immense emotional and financial drain on her, it led to the threat of imprisonment and to eventual bankruptcy. Thus the facts of Sylvia's life seem to portray a woman who, although living an unconventional lifestyle and taking extraordinary risks, still behaved in a traditionally female way: as the tireless, unpaid housekeeper to

male genius, the modest, self-effacing minister's daughter, and ultimate acquiescing victim of male greed.

Such a portrait only shows one side of Sylvia Beach. We know that she was an entertaining storyteller with a sharp, ironic wit and a knack for pantomime, and who, with no formal education, spoke four languages. Before settling in Paris, she had travelled throughout Europe, supporting the suffrage movement in Italy, writing articles such as "Spanish Feminism in 1916," and attracting much attention in her trousers and short hair in Touraine during the war.

After her death, Sylvia's friends wrote about her as a woman of intense loyalties and passions, who was strong-willed, intelligent and endlessly energetic: "Has anyone imagined that Sylvia's devotion to her chosen writers was selfless? She was a barbed-wire fence of self."[25]

Selfless or not, it seems that Sylvia leaned on Adrienne to set limits which she herself did not set on the demands of customers and friends. It was Adrienne who, in 1931, finally put a stop to Joyce's endless financial loans and emotional demands. At a time when Joyce had reached godlike stature, Adrienne wrote him a scathing letter exposing him as a manipulative fame-and-fortune-seeker, a letter Sylvia never would have written. In her memoirs, Sylvia Beach described the insanity of Joyce's demands during the publication of *Ulysses,* but it is impossible to know whether her lack of bitterness in the telling veiled, as Joyce himself assumed it did, unspoken hostility.

> … James Joyce and *Ulysses* had practically taken over the bookshop in the rue de l'Odéon. We attended to Joyce's correspondence, were his bankers, his agents, his errand boys … The printers, like everyone else connected with this great work, found out that it was invading their lives … They followed my orders to supply Joyce with all the proofs he wanted, and he was insatiable. Every proof was covered with additional text … Joyce told me he had written a third of *Ulysses* on the proofs.[26]

Janet Flanner celebrated the publication of *Ulysses* in her *New Yorker* column and described the excitement in Paris when the first copy

LEFT "I worshiped James Joyce," Sylvia confessed.

appeared in Shakespeare and Company's shop window, but bemoaned Joyce's unfair treatment of Sylvia:

> [Sylvia was like a] beast of burden struggling beneath the crushing load of a singular author's genius and egotisms, heavy as stones or marble in the case of the Dubliner Joyce ... All of Joyce's gratitude, largely unexpressed, should have been addressed to her as a woman. For the patience she gave him was female ... She always gave more than she received. Publishing *Ulysses* was her greatest act of generosity.[27]

The expression of Joyce's gratitude seems to have been limited to a short poem he wrote for Sylvia upon receiving the first copy of *Ulysses* on his fortieth birthday ("Who is Sylvia"), and a comment he made privately to a third party, "All she ever did was to make me a present of the ten best years of her life."[28] For her part, Sylvia did not see publishing the novel as a present or an act of generosity. The greatness of Joyce's work demanded sacrifices from everyone, herself especially, and she had little resentment about its emotional and financial cost to her personally:

> Up to the last minute, the long-suffering printers in Dijon were getting back these proofs, with new things to be inserted somehow, whole paragraphs even, dislocating pages. [They] suggested that I call Joyce's attention to the danger of going beyond my depth; perhaps his appetite for proofs might be curbed. But no, I wouldn't hear of such a thing. *Ulysses* was to be as Joyce wished, in every respect.
>
> I wouldn't advise "real" publishers to follow my example, nor authors to follow Joyce's. It would be the death of publishing. My case was different. It seemed natural to me that the efforts and sacrifices on my part should be proportionate to the greatness of the work I was publishing.[29]

Among Sylvia's sacrifices for *Ulysses* were two of her best customers. Gertrude Stein called at the shop one day to withdraw her support and announce that thereafter she would patronize the American Library on the Right Bank instead.

Sam Steward, a young American in Paris in the thirties who was close to Gertrude Stein, recalls that she "felt a little frozen out, or at

ABOVE: Gisèle Freund's portrait of James Joyce with his publishers, taken when relations between them were already strained.

ABOVE: Déjeuner Ulysses: A luncheon given in honor of the appearance of a French edition of *Ulysses,* published by Adrienne Monnier in 1929.

least a little wounded by the fact that Sylvia Beach had paid so much attention to the publication of Joyce's *Ulysses* and had not really done much about Gertrude's writing."[30]

But before long it was Sylvia who was frozen out. When Joyce became rich and famous, he thanked Sylvia by breaking their publishing contract and selling rights that belonged to her. According to Gisèle Freund,

> Hemingway was unknown. All these people [who later became the most famous writers of our century] were unknown. And they became known through Adrienne and Sylvia. To publish *Ulysses,* this was incredible! This Sylvia Beach did, and she went bankrupt, thanks to Joyce. She had not a penny left, nothing. And then he made a very big arrangement with an American publisher and forgot about the arrangement he had made with Sylvia Beach.[31]

Very late in the procedure (only six months before Adrienne's angry letter attempting to sever ties with him) Joyce produced a contract between himself and Sylvia, described by Janet Flanner as "a strange,

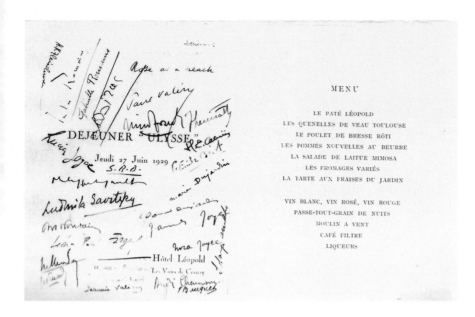

MENU

LE PATÉ LÉOPOLD
LES QUENELLES DE VEAU TOULOUSE
LE POULET DE BRESSE RÔTI
LES POMMES NOUVELLES AU BEURRE
LA SALADE DE LAITUE MIMOSA
LES FROMAGES VARIÉS
LA TARTE AUX FRAISES DU JARDIN

VIN BLANC, VIN ROSÉ, VIN ROUGE
PASSE-TOUT-GRAIN DE NUITS
MOULIN A VENT
CAFÉ FILTRE
LIQUEURS

ABOVE: Luncheon menu

Jesuitical document" which granted Sylvia world rights in *Ulysses.*
Contract in hand, she tried to sell the book to an American publisher,
Curtis Brown, who withdrew his offer when Sylvia requested what
she thought "a modest estimate of the value that *Ulysses* represents to
me." Sylvia confided to her sister, "It must be because of my sex that
they think I wouldn't charge them anything."[32] Joyce himself was
to violate the contract soon after; the next deal for an American edition he signed behind her back with Random House, and pocketed a
45,000-dollar advance. Sylvia called Joyce in anger and released him
from all of her claims to *Ulysses.*

Gertrude Stein was also angry about James Joyce, and it was more
than a matter of simple jealousy. She felt her book, *The Making of
Americans,* written almost two decades before *Ulysses* but not published until 1925, suffered unfairly from the ordeal that the printers
in Dijon had already undergone with *Ulysses.* Robert McAlmon, who
was publishing it through his Contact Editions, wrote to her,

> Neither Mr. Joyce or Miss Beach estimated rightly on the no.
> of words in *Ulysses* ... The work [Making of Americans] has
> stayed too long unpublished but the error made by my believ-
> ing Joyce knew how many words were in his book will of

ABOVE: *Le Navire d'Argent:* Adrienne's self-published journal, which included her own writings under a pseudonym.

course mean a great difference in the quotation I can expect from the printer. It will be almost double.[33]

The "long-suffering" printers in Dijon survived the two Modernist epics of the decade, *Ulysses* and *The Making of Americans,* only to have *Ulysses* return for publication in a French edition at the end of the decade. Adrienne Monnier was the novel's first French-language publisher, again no small task. The French novelist Valéry Larbaud, who thought *Ulysses* to be "as great as Rabelais," became its official translator. During the long, arduous publication process, Adrienne held a bilingual public reading by Larbaud and Joyce in her bookshop.

Although the business of the shop took most of her energy, Adrienne somehow managed to launch her own magazine, the short-lived *Navire d'Argent* (she later published the *Gazette des Amis des Livres* as well). In it she introduced in translation the work of English, American, and German writers to France. T.S. Eliot was speaking for many when he wrote that "to Adrienne Monnier, with *Navire d'Argent,* I owe the introduction of my verse to French readers,"[34] although Adrienne and Sylvia together had translated his "Love Song of J. Alfred Prufrock." Adrienne found the translation relatively easy, unlike *The Waste Land,* which she and Sylvia "would never have dared to attack." Adrienne also compiled and published the first bibliography of English literature available in French.

In the first issue of Adrienne's *Navire d'Argent* was a short monologue, "Homme buvant du vin," by J.-M. Sollier. The surname was Adrienne's mother's, and the pseudonym was her own. This was just

RIGHT: The publication of Adrienne's *Gazettes,* a volume of philosophical and critical essays about literature and politics, which she published under her own name.

LA MAISON DES AMIS DES LIVRES

7, RUE DE L'ODÉON, PARIS VIe

Nouvelle Direction : Jacques LAMY

Lundi 14 Décembre, de 16 à 19 heures
Adrienne Monnier signera son livre

Les Gazettes d'Adrienne Monnier

(Cette signature sera la seule faite par l'auteur)

Les personnes qui désirent des exemplaires sur bon papier *(voir prospectus ci-joint)* sont priés de les souscrire dès maintenant. Il sera réservé des exemplaires du premier tirage de l'édition courante sur demande faite à l'avance. Ecrire ou téléphoner : DAN. 07-41

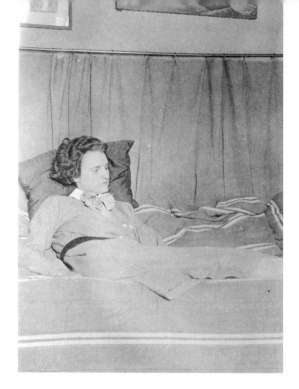

ABOVE: A quiet afternoon at home, when Sylvia still lived with Adrienne at 18, rue de l'Odéon, down the street from the two bookshops.

one of Adrienne's many prose pieces she later collected in a book and published herself. In *Navire's* final issue, devoted to poetry in May 1926, she included two poems of her own. According to Gisèle Freund, the pseudonym was a function of her femaleness:

> When she wrote a book under the name of her grandfather [her mother's maiden name], under the name of Sollier, everybody thought it was a marvelous book. It was a wonderful book until they heard it was Adrienne. The only writer who knew about it was Léon-Paul Fargue, and when he told the others this is Adrienne Monnier, all those who had thought it was wonderful became quiet. Nobody wanted to speak about it anymore because she was much more useful to the writers, to help them, to publish them, and as a seller of their books, than to write herself, which is what she always wanted. She did everything for other people. And this made her embittered. Today a woman would just do it but in those times, you see, she just couldn't do it ... [35]

If the need to hide her own authorship was particularly female, so was

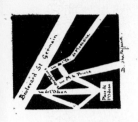

On " SHAKESPEARE AND COMPANY'S " bookshelves will be found not only the Classics, but the works of english and american authors of to-day, from Hardy, Shaw, Chesterton, Alice Meynell, Henry James, Edith Wharton... to the younger georgian and american authors.

Hitherto, french readers have encountered a certain difficulty in keeping in touch with recent movements across the Channel and on the other side of the Atlantic; but with the arrival upon the scene of " SHAKESPEARE AND COMPANY " that difficulty no longer exists.

— Henceforth, the french public will have an opportunity to follow closely in the newest reviews, anthologies, etc., the modern poetry and prose of England, Ireland and America.

SHAKESPEARE AND COMPANY
———— Sylvia Beach ————

8, Rue Dupuytren.- Paris (VI)

ABOVE: This bookmark, predating the move to rue de l'Odéon, is addressed to French readers interested in finding English-language books, although the majority of the customers in the twenties were English and American.

her literary style. Referring not to her poetry but to her "gazettes," the critic Jean Amrouche has written:

> Her art of telling is in close correspondence with her art of living. Her writings name, point out, evoke, paint, or describe real objects with which she had dealing and which life bore forth to her whose welcome always preceded the offering ... That took place, I saw it the way I am telling it, with the joy that I took in it, that is what clearly underlies most of the gazettes.[36]

Adrienne's literary style is almost too vibrant and sensual to fit under the category "criticism." In her essay "Lunch with Colette" the menu is virtually transformed from words on a page to tastes in one's mouth, both pleasant and not:

> Today there are snails. "Ah, no!" says Colette, "it's the only thing I've never been able to eat. I've tried to enjoy them, but nothing goes down except the juice." In my corner I exult, for I have a horror of snails, and I have never even wanted to put one of them in my mouth.

The dialogue Adrienne re-created from her lunch with Colette has that spontaneity and disorder of real life: one moment fortune-tellers, the next Colette's occasional "urge to kill" someone. Adrienne's words convey her *joie de vivre*—despite her living through poverty, world wars, and health torments that would eventually end her life in suicide.

Looking back on her life, Sylvia wrote that her three great loves had been Adrienne Monnier, James Joyce, and Shakespeare and Company. The first heartache accompanying these loves was the severing of her ties with Joyce, but within ten years Sylvia would also move out from Adrienne and lose Shakespeare and Company as well.

For the first time in twenty-two years, Sylvia went back to the United States in 1937 on the occasion of her father's eighty-fourth birthday. Her return was delayed by several months when she learned she needed a hysterectomy and then several weeks of rest. Upon her eventual return home, she discovered that Gisèle Freund had moved into her apartment and become more intimate with Adrienne. The refugee photographer had been taken in by them the previous winter and Adrienne had arranged a "marriage of convenience" for residency purposes; but now, as Shari Benstock put it, she "represented a threat to Sylvia's relationship with Adrienne."[37] Sylvia promptly moved across the street to live above her shop, but continued to eat her meals with Adrienne and Gisèle as her new apartment had no proper kitchen.

There were other reasons to continue meals with Adrienne. Bryher recalled that they were "a unique experience, first to eat the dinner because she cooked better than anyone whom I have ever known, and then to listen to the conversation of some of the finest minds in France … Sylvia, of course, had been adopted by them all."[38]

Sylvia turned her energies to salvaging the financially drained Shakespeare and Company, an effort to which her many friends, especially Bryher, rallied. According to Gisèle Freund, there were times when Sylvia would have died of hunger had it not been for Bryher. A check for 4,000 French francs arrived just at the point when Sylvia "was feeling like giving up the whole 'racket'!" She called Bryher her "wonderful fairy godmother."

As if the financial disaster of *Ulysses* were not enough, international events conspired to destroy her bookshop. Soon after the stock market crash of 1929, Sylvia began feeling the effects of the Depression: not only could customers afford fewer books, but there were far fewer customers. Although her clientele had always been international, the mainstay of her business was American expatriates, most of whom

LEFT: The contents of what had been Shakespeare and Company, including the sign above the premises, removed to a vacant apartment for safekeeping during the Occupation.

repatriated as soon as the dollar fell against the franc. She admitted to Bryher that her business was "practically at a standstill." Finally, in great sadness, she resorted to selling some of her treasured first editions and private manuscripts.

When Sylvia confided to André Gide that she might have to close down, it was the French writers from Adrienne's shop across the street who came to her rescue. They formed a committee of some of the most important writers of the day, and issued a successful subscription appeal. Expatriate stragglers also pitched in and Janet Flanner recalled that poetry readings helped to gain new subscribers:

> Valéry recited some of his most beautiful poems — including "Le Serpent," at Joyce's special request, although no mention is made of Joyce's reading anything … T.S. Eliot came over from London to give a reading, and even Hemingway consented to read aloud from his works when Stephen Spender agreed to make it a double bill. And so Shakespeare and Company was saved …[39]

But it was only a short reprive. Sylvia lost her third great love in 1941 when a German officer in occupied Paris insisted on buying her personal copy of *Finnegans Wake.* Several times previously she had thought the time had come when she would have to close the shop, but she had survived each crisis and ignored her father's pleas to return to America. When France entered the war, it was her government who pleaded. Sylvia somehow "had resisted all efforts of my embassy to persuade me to return to the United States … Instead, I had settled down to share life in Nazi-occupied Paris with my friends."[40] But when Sylvia refused to sell her private copy, the officer threatened to return and confiscate all her books. That afternoon, Sylvia, with the help of Adrienne and her concierge, emptied out thousands of books, letters, pictures, as well as the tables and chairs, carrying them up four flights to a vacant apartment and safety. Sylvia painted over the bookshop sign on the building, and within two hours Shakespeare and Company had disappeared.

The Nazis did come back another time to arrest Sylvia and place her in an internment camp with other expatriate Americans who dared to stay in their adopted homeland. But the remains of what had been Shakespeare and Company were never found; they survived as a hidden treasure until the liberation of Paris.

ABOVE: Occupied Paris

2

THE WRITER AND HER MUSE

In September 1907, Gertrude and Alice first met in Paris where they would remain, together, for the next four decades. In *The Autobiography of Alice B. Toklas*, Gertrude described their meeting, presumably as she wanted Alice to have experienced it:

> I was impressed by the coral brooch she wore and by her voice. I may say that only three times in my life have I met a genius and each time a bell within me rang and I was not mistaken ... The three geniuses of whom I wish to speak are Gertrude Stein, Pablo Picasso and Alfred Whitehead.

Alice herself described her first impressions of Gertrude with even more adulation:

> She was large and heavy with delicate small hands and a beautifully modeled and unique head ... She had a certain physical beauty and enormous power ... I was impressed with her presence and her wonderful eyes and beautiful voice—an incredibly beautiful voice ... Her voice had the beauty of a singer's voice when she spoke.[1]

LEFT: The writer and her muse.

One Sunday evening in the winter of 1908, Gertrude Stein was writing at the large wooden table in her studio. The

ABOVE: "We were so wifely."

walls around her were crammed with peculiar, nonsensical paintings. Wearing her usual writing garb of a monk-like brown robe, she suddenly stood up, gathered up her papers and rushed out of the room. She hurried into the kitchen, pausing only to catch a savory whiff of her dinner cooking on the stove. Gertrude loved good food, and especially Alice's American cooking, but even more she loved her own writing—which Katherine Anne Porter has called "no doubt the dearest of Miss Stein's possessions."[2] Full of excitement, Gertrude told Alice, "You'll have to take whatever you're cooking off the stove so it won't burn or stop cooking it entirely for you must read this."[3]

It was neither poem, novel, nor play she had just finished but rather "Ada"—a word-portrait, the first of dozens she would write throughout her lifetime. She invented this literary form out of the deep affinity she felt with the Cubist portraits of her artist friends, particularly Picasso. Her friendships served as a wellspring of her writing; her word-portraits, written between 1908 and 1946, were tributes to great friendships with "ordinary" mortals as well as with such luminaries as Raoul Dufy, Marcel Duchamp, Francis Picabia, Isadora Duncan, Sherwood Anderson, Hemingway, Cézanne, Max Jacob, Juan Gris, Francis Rose, Picasso, Matisse, Man Ray, Edith Sitwell, and Madame de Clermont-Tonnerre.

THE WRITER AND HER MUSE

Many of these individuals weren't yet famous when Gertrude wrote about them, and many of the portraits weren't of famous people at all. The question of fame was something Gertrude considered of no importance, either in her friendships or her word-portraits. What mattered in the word-portraits even more than the personality of the subject was the vitality and essence of her writing. Gertrude saved and cherished a comment published in the *Sunday Observer* in 1939 that claimed that Joyce's style in *Finnegans Wake* had "its precedents in Lewis Carroll and Gertrude Stein, who was the first, so far as I know, in her 'Portrait of Mabel Dodge,' to strive for a new effect from the contortions of grammar and syntax."

The story of Alice putting dinner on hold to listen to Gertrude's first "word-portrait" gives us an insight into Alice's importance, already secure a year after they had met, as Gertrude's confidante, intended reader, muse, editor, memory prod for incidents and events, and even virtual "collaborator" (Alice's creative deciphering of Gertrude's illegible scrawl, and her correction of Gertrude's mistakes or introduction of new textual errors raises interesting questions of authorship).

Had Alice performed her literary services for a great man, it is likely she'd only now be recognized as a subject fit for rescue from obscurity by a literary biographer. But unlike a conventional wife, Alice was allowed to occupy a central role in Gertrude's writing and public life so that she lives on in our collective cultural memory while the wives of Gertrude's male contemporaries, such as Picasso, Hemingway, or Ezra Pound, remain largely unknown to us.

Like the rest of the world, Gertrude Stein believed genius to be male. In her early, unpublished notebooks, Gertrude wrote of the artist Elie Nadelman:

> Nadelman, like Pablo and Matisse have a maleness that belongs
> to genius … Pure passion concentrated to the point of vision.

If maleness belongs to genius, where did that leave Gertrude Stein? After such confident pronouncements about Picasso and Matisse she wrote more tentatively, "moi aussi perhaps." She interpreted maleness as a social role rather than biological essence, thus not excluding herself from the province of genius. In her relationship with Alice, she assumed the more conventionally male role, or, as Catharine R.

Stimpson describes it, "As they violated the rules of sex, they obeyed those of gender."[4]

Yet Gertrude's writing was not so obedient, and took on a playful fluidity of gender. In "Didn't Nelly and Lilly Love You" (1922), the story of Gertrude's and Alice's birthplaces and their meeting in Paris starts out with the polarized "he" and "she" and ends up with the more ambiguous "we" and "I":

> … It was a coincidence that he moved there and that she stayed there and that they were and that he became to be there and she came not to be fair, she was darker than another, how can a sky be pale and how can a lily be so common that it makes a hedge. I do know that she never met him there … We never met … Now actually what happened was this. She was born in California and he was born in Allegheny, Pennsylvania.
> … I love her with an a because I say that she is not afraid. How can I tell you of the meeting.
> … She came late I state that she came late and I said what was it that I said I said I am not accustomed to wait. We were so wifely.

The resulting ambiguity could be maddening to some, as it was to Natalie Barney, who nonetheless realized that Gertrude's "obscurity" functioned as "the better part of discretion." Gertrude's seemingly opaque style made possible her "improper" and audacious subject matter, so carefully disguised at times that the lesbian center of her writing was never fathomed. Having read steadily through "Didn't Nelly and Lilly Love You," Natalie Barney claimed she couldn't "make out whether they did or didn't—the chances being two against one they didn't."[5]

Behind the ever-shifting pronouns lurk Gertrude's fears and doubts about identity, her own and everyone else's. Her own family identity she considered a nuisance, while recognition by her little dog was reason enough to know "I am I." Later she even doubted this: "I became worried about identity … I was not sure but that that only proved the dog was he and not that I was I." When she told Alice that it is impossible for anyone to know oneself for sure, Alice, not plagued by such worries, answered, "That depends on who you are."[6]

Gertrude wrestled with what she called "the subject of identity" to the end of her life. In her last work, *The Mother of Us All*, she wrote of

ABOVE: "Slowly and in a way it was not astonishing but slowly I was knowing that I was a genius . . . It is funny this thing of being a genius, there is no reason for it, there is no reason that it should be you . . ." — *Everybody's Autobiography*

her heroine, Susan B., "I have had to be what I have had to be. I could never be one of two I could never be two in one as married couples do and can, I am but one all one, one and all one …"

This was only partially true of Susan B. Anthony (who spent much of her life with the married Elizabeth Cady Stanton), but it was particularly untrue of Gertrude. Gertrude may have had to be what she had to be, but she was always one of two, or even more so two in one. Her writing and Alice's "wifely" role as nurturer and caretaker were inseparable, interdependent entities, much as Gertrude and Alice were. In one of Gertrude's notebooks, she intermingled their names, coming up with "Gertrice/Altrude." Another notebook has a draft of an essay in her own hand on one page, with a shopping list in French in Alice's hand on the next. Alice's list also includes, in English, some crucial household tasks, such as taking their poodle Basket to the "farmacy." The daily tasks outlined in Alice's unself-conscious writing, and undertaken solely by her, made possible Gertrude's self-conscious writing on the next page, which, appropriately enough, Gertrude titled "how to write."

Even more than as caretaker, Alice served as muse and inspiration for Gertrude. Catharine R. Stimpson writes, "Stein wrote both out of and about her immediate world. Toklas supplied that world with raw material: events, tales, domestic details, tension, sexuality, and flair. Stein returned those materials to her as comparatively finished texts."[7] Gertrude's notebooks are filled with doodlings and private expressions in the margins around her manuscripts, revealing her subconscious and liminal preoccupations. In the notebook that holds the manuscript to *An American in France,* she made a line drawing of two figures resembling herself and Alice; opposite it she wrote:

> Prime de Merit
> I love she
> She is adorably we.
> When it is she
> She is me.
> She embroiders
> beautifully.

On the last page of this notebook, it was more than Alice's embroidery to which Gertrude paid tribute:

Tongue like a whip.
Dear little tongue.
Red little tongue.
Long little tongue.
Let little be mine.
[in very small, faint letters:]
yes yes yes

These private musings came to Gertrude in the middle of other literary endeavors—virtually all of which were *also* tributes to Alice—indicating that Alice as lover and muse was never far removed from Gertrude's creative process. Occasionally these marginal scrawls were sufficiently distracting from the manuscript at hand for them to move to central prominence. In her notebook for "Why I Do Not Live in America" written in July–August 1928 for publication in *transition* magazine, Gertrude drew in pencil a primitive rosebud vase, underneath which she wrote: "A vase of flowers for my rosebud." The rosebud theme stayed in her mind, for a few papers later she interrupted her treatise on America to write in big letters across two pages a poem which was to become famous—without, however, its revealing last line:

A
ROSE IS A
ROSE IS A
ROSE IS A
ROSE
She is my rose.

Judy Grahn, in *Really Reading Gertrude Stein,* tells us that these lines are usually misunderstood:

Large numbers of the reading public ... believe she meant that roses are tedious, tiresomely all alike, when she meant the opposite, that every time you see a rose it is a different experience because it is located at a different place in the "sentence" of your life; and moreover that a rose "is," has existence beyond our clichés about it.[8]

Gertrude created new relations between words, even between the same words. She did not call this repetition, but rather insistence, since through the repeating, meanings change.

She used words, not to describe the world around her, but to reproduce that world in language and sound. Consequently, her writing seemed more and more abstract, to the point where many could not follow her. Among them was her friend Natalie Barney although she was willing to give Gertrude the benefit of the doubt. Years later she wrote, referring to Gertrude, "we must be patient with geniuses, as they are most patient with themselves, and follow themselves even where we cannot follow them."[9] Bryher was more sure of the benefits of Gertrude's experimentation with language: "Her attack on language was necessary and helped us all, even if we did not follow her."[10]

One afternoon Gertrude Stein and Alice Toklas strolled down the rue de Rennes, which was lined with junk shops and antique dealers as it still is today. Gertrude was struck by a group of Spanish porcelain figures in a shop window, centering around what she thought was St. Ignatius. Despite her love of modern art, Gertrude's tastes ran towards the kitsch. Alice contradicted her about St. Ignatius, and claimed it may not even be Spanish, but suggested they buy it nonetheless. Suddenly Gertrude didn't want it anymore, especially if it wasn't as she first saw it. "I've got it inside me now and it would only interfere," she answered.

> Who makes it be what they had as porcelain.
> Saint Ignatius and left and right laterally be lined.
> All Saints.
>   To Saints.
> Four Saints
>   And Saints.
> Five Saints.
>   To Saints.
> Last Act.
> Which is a fact.

The porcelain figures found their way into the opera *Four Saints in Three Acts* which Gertrude Stein wrote in collaboration with composer Virgil Thomson and designer/painter Florine Stettheimer. It premiered, with an all-black cast, to rave reviews in New York in

30166

Indications de Service

M LC MISS GERTRUDE STEIN 27
RUE DE FLEURUS PARIS =

Timbre date

VIA RADIO-FRANCE

RFK 744 NEWYORK 14 9 2335
AINTS TRULY HEAVENLY =

MACPHERSON BRYHER +

ABOVE: Bryher was in the United States for the premiere of *Four Saints in Three Acts*. She later wrote, "The evening remains for me one of the most triumphant nights that I ever spent watching a stage ... Gertrude's text soared out magnificently and with it her, and our, rebellion against outworn art."

1934. One way or another, Gertrude used and transformed virtually everything she experienced.

Some of Gertrude's contemporaries found her transformations easier than others; not surprisingly, they were most often writers themselves. What *is* surprising is that the American writer William Carlos Williams, who seems to have generally despised the women in the Left Bank Modernist community, was one of her most vocal supporters. He wrote a "Manifesto" in defense of Gertrude's work, which he believed to be "in many ways of all American literary works the most modern." He appreciated her "revolutionary" approach to words themselves, detached from their associations in the world:

> The feeling is of words themselves, a curious immediate quality quite apart from their meaning ... It is simply the skeleton, the "formal" parts of writing, those that make form, that she has to do with, apart from the "burden" which they carry ... It is a revolution of some proportions that is contemplated the exact nature of which may be no more than sketched here but whose basis is humanity in a relationship with literature hitherto little contemplated ...[11]

Ernest Hemingway, a young reporter for the *Toronto Star* in the early 1920s, was another devotee of Gertrude's. He would trade on his

ABOVE: Gertrude collaborated with composer Virgil Thomson on
Four Saints. He claimed that that "her discovery of the opera as a
poetic form" was a result of her friendship with him.

BELOW Virgil Thomson's tribute to Gertrude Stein. He also wrote a
composition for Alice B. Toklas.

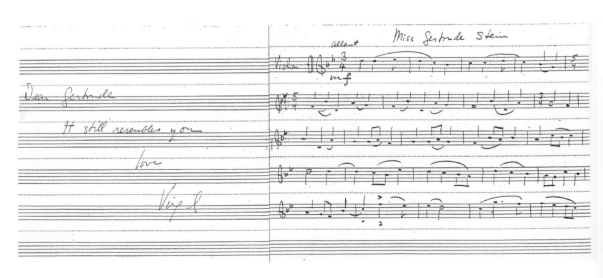

association with her ("Gertrude Stein and me are just like brothers") to enhance his own literary reputation. His letters to her in the early days of their friendship reveal a mentor/pupil relationship:

November 9, 1923

I am going to chuck journalism I think. You ruined me as a journalist last winter. Have been no good since … I've thought a lot about the things you said about working and am starting that way at the beginning. If you think of anything else I wish you'd write it to me. Am working hard about creating and keep my mind going about it all the time.

Within a year he had given up journalism altogether and was writing fiction. He wrote to Gertrude in August 1924, "I have finished two long short stories, one of them not much good, and the other very good … but isn't writing a hard job though? It used to be easy before I met you …"

Kenneth Macpherson, who edited the little magazine *Close-Up* with Bryher, was also among the small circle of those who had an appreciation of Gertrude's work. When writing to solicit some of her work for his magazine, he acknowledged that, "I consider that you have done more toward the advancement of thought in art than almost any other writer. Apart from which, one derives a real and stimulating pleasure from your writing." Shortly afterwards, he wrote again: "I must say that your writing and your feeling for words always seemed to me brilliant and inspired. I so hope you will send more, and very soon, and also frequently …"

Such a request for more work, even by the 1920s, is unique among Gertrude's vast correspondence with editors and publishers who, over the years, came up with increasingly creative epistles in trying to reject, yet again, the manuscripts she relentlessly submitted. In two of the earliest of such letters, the editors are simply stumped:

Duffield and Co., Publishers, August 14, 1906

Dear Miss Stein:

… we hardly see our way clear to making you any offer of publication of "Three Histories." The book is too

Works: *Ferrestone Press, West Norwood*

**/K.W.

NEW YORK
AND MELBOURNE

Telephone: 6111 Central.
Telegrams: "Franalmer, Fleet, London."

Frank Palmer,
Publisher.

14, Red Lion Court,
Fleet Street,
London, E.C.

27th January, 1913.

Dear Madam,

    I have read through a portion of the MS which you gave me on Friday, but I regret that I cannot make you any proposition concerning the same. I say I have only read a portion of it, because I found it perfectly useless to read further, as I did not understand any of it. I have to confess to being as stupid and as ignorant as all the other readers to whom the book has been submitted.

    I herewith return the MS.

        Yours faithfully,

        for Frank Palmer.

Miss Gertrude Stein,
      Knightsbridge Hotel,
         Knightsbridge, S.W.

unconventional, for one thing, and if I may say so, too literary
… This, at any rate, would be our unfavorable prognosis.

Sidgwick and Jackson, Ltd., London. January 29, 1913

Dear Madam,

We are returning herewith your MS. entitled "MANY MANY
WOMEN," as we are unable to offer to publish it for you.

    Under ordinary circumstances we should like to recommend
another publisher to whom the work might appeal; but we
regret to say that we do not think it probable that you will find
any publisher for work of this kind …

The rejection letters continued throughout the 1910s and '20s, but
without further confessions to being stupid or "at sea." By the mid-
1920s, it was the ignorant readers rather than publishers who were to
blame. In London, Jonathan Cape doubted "sufficient sales," while in
New York, Alfred Knopf "frankly [didn't] believe that we have progressed enough, even though you think we have, in modern literature
to make [publication] possible …"

    And so the publishing world rejected Gertrude Stein, but only after
she herself had dismissed the values of the entire literary establish-
ment. During the rebellious spirit of the twenties, the rejections may
have actually enhanced her reputation; Bryher recalled that, "If a manuscript was sold to an established publisher, its author was regarded
as a black sheep and for his own safety moved to the Right Bank."[12]
Although Gertrude did not write for fame or recognition, the decades
without it did take their toll. Many years after her death, her friend,
the Russian painter Pavel Tchelitchew, reflected on what this isolation
must have meant to Gertrude:

If you realized that she worked insistently, every day, to be
published the first time by a real publisher, publishing house,
after she was sixty. But I wonder who will do that, who will
have the insistence, you understand, the obsession, the surety,
the purity of insistence to do that. No concessions. She used to

MATISSE PICASSO

AND GERTRUDE STEIN

WITH

TWO SHORTER STORIES

BY

GERTRUDE STEIN

Directors
HERBERT JONATHAN CAPE
G. WREN HOWARD
Telephone
MUSEUM 9011, two lines

JONATHAN CAPE LIMITED
Publishers
THIRTY BEDFORD SQUARE
LONDON W.C.1

Telegrams
CAPAJON, WESTCENT
LONDON
Marconigrams
CAPAJON, LONDON

Nov.2oth.25.

Miss G.Stein,
27 rue de Fleurus,
Paris.

Dear Madam:-

We are sorry to return your MS "G.M.P."
without being able to make you an offer for its
publication. We fear, however, that we could not
make sufficient sales for it to satisfy you or
ourselves. Tnanking you,

We are,

Yours very truly,
Jonathan Cape Ltd.

ABOVE: When no one would publish Gertrude's *G.M.P,* Alice printed 500 copies herself, with the initials of the title spelled out and rearranged.

tell me, "Don't you ever dare to make concessions. Then one walks down, down, down, down."[13]

Even after she received her long awaited recognition in her sixties, she continued to give young novelists the same advice she gave Tchelitchew as a young man: "Let nothing else get in but that clear vision which you are alone with. If you have an audience it's not art. If anyone hears you it's no longer pure."[14]

But it is one matter to have an audience in your head while writing and quite another to have an audience reading your work when finished. Out of unwavering confidence and belief in Gertrude, not to mention sheer frustration, Alice started publishing the works herself in 1930. She established a press, Plain Edition, and extended her job as Gertrude's personal typist and editor into being her publisher as well. They financed the press with their reluctant sale of a Picasso:

> When Gertrude could not find a publisher she sold the beautiful Picasso painting of the girl with the fan held in the air, which quite broke my heart. And when she told Picasso, it made me cry. But it made it possible to publish the Plain Edition.[15]

Had Gertrude Stein not collected Picasso's paintings in the early twentieth century, she would not have been able to finance her own work twenty years later. And were it not for Gertrude Stein, it is possible that Picasso's paintings might still have been unsalable in 1930, much as her writings were. Twenty-five years earlier, Janet Flanner reminds us,

> Gertrude Stein, rich in enthusiasm but modest in means, and then about as unknown as a writer as Picasso was as a painter, began her famous and eclectic Picasso collection and her friendship with him, which over the years have been two of the most important personal elements in the Picasso legend. For her first Picasso, she and her brother Leo paid Sagot the art merchant 150 francs and all three quarreled about the picture's merits.
>
> It was the early, exquisite, conventional nude, "A Little Girl with Basket of Flowers." Miss Stein, who was already ripe to prefer stranger sights in art, thought the girl looked classically flat-footed ... After Miss Stein became close friends with

Picasso, she bought directly from him. She says that from 1906 to 1909 the Stein family controlled the Picasso output, since no one else wanted it.[16]

It wasn't difficult to maintain this control: neither had much money and often Picasso would trade a painting for some eggs or would barter with her for other essentials. When Gertrude fell in love with Cézanne's portrait of Mme. Cézanne wearing an extraordinary green dress, she bought it outright, much to the annoyance of her family who thought she must be mad. As Gertrude came into a bit more money, she began to collect paintings by Juan Gris and Picabia, also not yet in demand.

Even today, art historians have a hard time crediting Gertrude Stein for her visionary role in modern art, although the paintings she selected were eventually to be scooped up by the Museum of Modern Art in New York. Most like to claim it was Leo Stein rather than his younger sister Gertrude who first recognized Picasso's genius. Biographers with an inexplicable anti–Gertrude Stein bias often suggest that her admiration for Picasso was not reciprocated, despite evidence of their friendship. Picasso named Gertrude and Alice the godparents of his child (as did Hemingway) and by 1919 had begun to give Gertrude paintings as ironically, such was his success that she could no longer afford to buy them. In the mid-twenties, Picasso surprised Gertrude by making etchings for a forthcoming limited edition of her "Birthday-Book," which she had written for his son.

Granted, Gertrude Stein was not alone in "discovering" Picasso: the poets Max Jacob and Guillaume Apollinaire also championed his work. But Gertrude and Leo, and then Gertrude and Alice, collected his paintings while others only laughed at them. According to Pavel Tchelitchew, Gertrude "was the one who discovered great French painters. She and her brothers paid their attention to Matisse in old good days when Matisse was unknown … Then Gertrude Stein discovered Picasso … She was the one who had believed in him. She was the one whom he painted. She was really his great friend and protector."[17]

Their important and volatile friendship continued for over four decades, from 1905 to Gertrude's death. Fame cost Picasso most of his other early friendships but it never came between the two. Although neither spoke nor read the other's mother tongue, they seemed to understand each other implicitly. Gertrude always felt that there was a "particularly strong sympathy between Picasso and myself as to modern direction."[18] During one of the eighty or ninety sittings for Picasso's portrait of her, she mentioned that she heard with her eyes and saw with her ears. Picasso immediately agreed to this method.[19]

Whether it was his ears or his eyes that were responsible, none of their friends thought the portrait resembled Gertrude. "Never mind," Picasso replied, "in the end she will manage to look just like it." He was upset when she cut her hair—"and my portrait!" was his response.

Picasso and Gertrude became especially close during these sittings for the now famous portrait. Every Saturday, he and his lover Fernande would walk Gertrude home across Paris and stay for dinner. These weekly meals coincided with the beginning of the informal salons. Gertrude wrote,

> Little by little people began to come to the rue de Fleurus to see the Matisses and the Cézannes, Matisse brought people, everybody brought somebody, and they came at any time and it began to be a nuisance, and it was in this way that Saturday evenings began.

Soon, meeting Gertrude Stein would be considered a rite of passage into the Modernist movement. Janet Flanner, who was frequently there, recalled,

> Her studio was the most fascinating of any place in Paris, because everyone did go there, about once a week she'd have a tea party ... And she always led the conversation, well Gertrude led everything ... When she laughed everyone in the room laughed. It was more than a signal, it was a contagion of good spirits.... While Gertrude orated and made the pattern of the conversation, Miss Alice B. Toklas was sitting behind a tea tray. It was as if Gertrude was giving the address and Alice was supplying all the corrective footnotes.[20]

It has become legendary that the wives were restricted to hearing the corrective footnotes. Although Janet "always thought behind the tea tray was the best place to be," the segregated arrangement particularly annoyed Sylvia Beach, even though she was not a wife herself: "I knew the rules and regulations about wives at Gertrude's. They couldn't be kept from coming, but Alice had strict orders to keep them out of the way while Gertrude conversed with the husbands ... I couldn't see the necessity for the cruelty."[21] But then Sylvia was very defensive about wives. In a letter to Bryher, who had asked if any women would be attending a "famous reception" she and Adrienne had organized for French writers, she answered,

> I was amused and interested to see in your letter to Adrienne that you would have liked to see what women were being invited, if any. All have wives and will be accompanied by same, and very fine wives they are, mostly. But aside from the two brilliant exceptions of Colette and Adrienne Monnier, I can't mention a single woman writer in France to-day [i.e. French] who is any good. That's the plain truth.... There is nothing to compare with the English and American women writers. Strange, isn't it.

If Sylvia and Adrienne surrounded themselves with writers, Gertrude "attracted and influenced not only writers but painters, musicians, and least but not last, disciples," according to Natalie Barney. "She, instead of offering helpless sympathy, often helped them out, by changing an *idée fixe* or obsession into a fresh start in a new direction."[22] In this way Gertrude advised and supported many young artists and writers who went on to become famous.

Some, but not all, would be grateful to Gertrude for this help and encouragement for the rest of their lives. Pavel Tchelitchew was one:

> I am very pleased to come to talk to you about Gertrude Stein. She was my great friend, in fact I owe her everything that happened to me since the time I met her. Because from a very obscure person I suddenly became a young artist on whom there was put a spot of light ... I liked Gertrude Stein because there was something in her extremely friendly, extremely good, extremely maternal, and something like somebody one has always known ...[23]

Gertrude Stein is so often likened to a man among men at these salons, while Alice is the wife surrounded by other wives, that Pavel Tchelitchew's choice of the word "maternal" leaps out as incongruous

ABOVE "Group of Artists" by Marie Laurencin, 1908. "In the early days Marie Laurencin painted a strange picture, portraits of Guillaume [Apollinaire], Picasso, Fernande and herself. Fernande told Gertrude Stein about it. Gertrude Stein bought it and Marie Laurencin was so pleased. It was the first picture of hers any one had ever bought." — from *The Autobiography of Alice B. Toklas*

and even suspect. But most of the men surrounding Gertrude at her salon were homosexual, and much younger than she. According to Sam Steward, a young homosexual who befriended her in the 1930s,

> … the ladies generally were entertained by Alice and talked to her about recipes and "female" things. Whereas Gertrude liked to talk with the men who were present, the husbands, and the young homosexual writers and artists that flocked to Gertrude and were her most devoted fans and admirers.[24]

Pavel Tchelitchew and his partner Allen Tanner were two of the many young men who admired Gertrude. Others included the English painter Francis Rose, American photographer George Platt Lynes, the French writer René Crevel, German photographer Horst P. Horst, composer and writer Paul Bowles, and the choreographer Frederick Ashton (who choreographed Gertrude Stein's "The Wedding Bouquet" and performed it at Sadlers Wells in London in 1937).

Gertrude did pay attention to women at the salon, but only if they weren't also wives. Samuel Putnam recalled that, contrary to legend, "it is also my impression that there were more women than men among Stein's devotees. What moral there is to this, I am sure I do not know; but if one is to judge from the reports brought back, she appeared to get on better with the women ..."[25] Edith Sitwell was always flattered that Gertrude was respectful toward her at the salons as she had heard that women were treated as Alice's visitors. Marie Laurencin, although the "mistress" of poet Guillaume Apollinaire before the First World War, was respected by Gertrude as an extraordinary artist in her own right. She attended the salon regularly, Gertrude bought some of her paintings, and, despite an interlude of coolness following the publication of Gertrude's *Autobiography of Alice B. Toklas,* the two women remained friends until Gertrude's death.

Like Janet Flanner, Bryher preferred Alice's company at the salons, and would slip away from Gertrude to join Alice's conversation. Although on occasion Gertrude requested of Bryher that they talk over certain literary ideas, Bryher felt she could not offer Gertrude sufficient intellectual stimulus. And, furthermore, she only admired Gertrude whereas she loved Alice.

Picasso relished in the international flavor and sexual ambiguity of the gatherings. According to his biographer John Richardson, Picasso "was used to seeing Gertrude in the company of other emancipated women."[26] The salon conversations were scintillating, in part because Gertrude was always at the center of them, and in part because the guests did not get progressively drunk and mentally impaired. One of the salon regulars recalled that this was in marked "difference with my other American friends who used to go in cafés, drinking cocktails and

LEFT: Painter Marie Laurencin was a regular at Gertrude and Alice's salon.

discussing and discussing till they didn't know what they were talking about [while Gertrude] was having teas ..."27 Gertrude herself did not find this café life interesting. She wrote, "Drinkers think each other are amusing but that is only because they are both drunk. It is funny the two things most men are proudest of is the thing that any man can do and doing does in the same way, that is being drunk and being the father of their son."

Four years after Gertrude sat for Picasso's famous portrait, she began writing her own portrait of Picasso. After unsuccessfully submitting it to several journals, together with her portrait of Matisse, Gertrude Stein found a publisher in the New York photographer and art collector Alfred Stieglitz. Stieglitz accepted the portraits for his magazine *Camera Work* in 1913, and printed them alongside reproductions of paintings by Picasso and Matisse.

The following year, *The New York Times,* to Gertrude's delight, dubbed her a "Cubist of Letters." But the publisher Alfred A. Knopf, then at Doubleday, responded thus to the *Camera Work* experiment:

Dear Mr. Stieglitz —

Thank you for the Stein issue. I can see many possible causes for the lady's spasms but none for their publication ...—tho I know nothing of Matisse and Picasso but the pictures in *Camera Work:* perhaps they could only be explained thru such spasms as G.S. had gone thru. I don't object to her doing what she did but I do object to having to see it in print! at any rate when unadorned by any apologies or explanations on her part.

Knopf must have come to regret this letter, even if he never came to see any value whatsoever in "This one always had something coming out of this one. This one was working. This one always had been working. This one was always having something that was coming out of this one."

Gertrude did not respond to Knopf; indeed, she rarely answered her detractors, however strange their criticisms seemed to her. She believed, "Being intelligible is not what it seems. Everybody has their own English ... You will see, they will understand it. If you enjoyed it, then you understand it."28

Stieglitz, who ran a gallery in New York, was along with critic

Henry McBride among the first in the United States to acknowledge the Modernist movement in art. Henry McBride, considered the "dean of American art critics," came to appreciate the work of Picasso, Matisse, Braque, and Léger through his association with Gertrude Stein, whom he often went to visit in Paris.

The letters between Gertrude Stein and Henry McBride constitute an informal history of modern art and artists. Early on, Gertrude promised to "let you know if anything new creeps up in Paris in the art way …" During the First World War Gertrude gave McBride an informal report on the activities of all the artists they admired. After chastising him for his briefly pro-German stance, she asked, "Perhaps you would like to know about the painters." She listed their itineraries:

> Braque is at the front in the trenches. Derain is an Incidist but
> so far has been laid up with a leg. Apollinaire is in training to
> be a conductor of cannon and is incidentally learning to ride
> and getting fat … Picabia is driving an automobile. Delaunay is
> so to speak not a patriot. All the Americans are red cross and
> are working hard at it in a most engaging uniform. I guess
> that's all …

Gertrude herself was among those in an engaging Red Cross uniform, as was Alice, Sylvia Beach, and many other American women. Gertrude and Alice drove around the countryside in their Ford truck, which they named Auntie, dispensing supplies to French war hospitals and later doubling as an ambulance service. Alice recalled that

> There were no official agencies … You were Americans helping
> the French, so you appealed to Americans. Well, I appealed to
> my father. He was very good. His Club sent an ambulance
> when we wanted it and sent an x-ray apparatus … Our sup-
> plies all came from private people … comforts and bandages,
> and surgical instruments and things of that kind.[29]

Gertrude and Alice distributed these supplies and the only arguments ever witnessed between them were sparked by Gertrude's efforts to park the truck.

In a letter of November 1915, Gertrude wrote, "There is no use talking about the war it is not fit to talk about." But she did talk—and write—about the war, during it and for years afterwards. Among her

ABOVE: After World War One, Alice found that Paris "like us was sadder than when we left it," although Gertrude was proud to receive this certificate.

pieces were "Accents in Alsace" and "The Deserter," both rejected by *Harper's, Everybody's Magazine,* and other publications. Nonetheless, meeting all sorts of people through her war work made her more convinced that there were readers for her work, if only she could reach them. "Accents in Alsace" is a political satire, but like everything else Gertrude wrote, it is really about Alice: "In me meeney miney mo. You are my love and I tell you so."

Gertrude was never savvy about politics and often made stupid, even reactionary comments for which she is ridiculed to this day. But she lived through and wrote intimately about the horrors of war; indeed, it became one of her strongest themes. When the German army entered Paris during World War II, Gertrude and Alice escaped to their summer home in the South, and it is said that their entire village conspired to keep the presence of the two American Jews there a secret.

Wars I Have Seen documents her observations through the two world wars. In it she addresses large political questions, such as why statesmen declare war, not as a political theorist would but with the simplicity and directness of a child:

> they are still believing what they are supposed to believe
> nobody else believes it, not even all their families believe it but
> believe it or not, they still do believe it ... And so naturally
> they believing what they are supposed to believe make it
> possible for the country to think they can win a war ...

When she drops her childlike observations in favor of political analysis—for example she "always thought [Pétain] was right to make the armistice [with Germany]"—she clearly overreaches her grasp. But she is in full command when she moves from broad, rambling storytelling to sudden, unnerving personal detail:

> And now in June 1943, it is trying, there are so many sad
> things happening, so many in prison, so many going away, our
> dentist's son and he was only eighteen and he should have been
> taking his entrance university examinations and he with others
> in a camion took shoes and clothes and weapons to give to the
> young men who had taken themselves to the mountains, to
> avoid being sent away, and what has happened to him and
> to them.

Novelist Richard Wright defended Gertrude's writing ever since his "ears were opened" by *Three Lives* "for the first time to the magic of the spoken word. I began to hear the speech of my grandmother, who spoke a deep, pure Negro dialect ..." Richard Wright remained a loyal reader of what he called "Steinian prose" and reviewed *Wars I Have Seen*: "I know of no current war book that conveys a more awful sense of the power of war to kill the soul, of the fear, the rumor, the panic, and the uncertainty of war."[30]

At the war's end, Gertrude Stein turned her home into a beckoning harbor for American soldiers adrift in a sea of fear, panic, and uncertainty. If she was too old to provide the material support she had given to French soldiers during the First World War, her emotional support for American soldiers during the Second may have been equally significant. Learning of her death the following year, one soldier wrote to Alice,

> Dear Miss Toklas:
>
> You may remember me as the sergeant named Billy who used to come to your house last summer to talk ...
>
> It seems that everyone in this country has had their say about Miss Stein; and it must be gratifying ... — to see how much she meant emotionally as well as intellectually to her country, and to see how quickly she has become a genuine American legend.
>
> I have no special articulateness or perception and ... merely wanted to tell you how much you both did for so many of us who were just emerging from bitter experiences. We thought of your home as an outpost of all we could take pride in; you both made us feel a special excitement and obligation in just being Americans; and you both gave us something to hold us against the flood of disillusion that follows any victory ...
> Sincerely William C. Haygood [Chicago]

Gertrude had become particularly patriotic during the Second World War, although she had always identified strongly with being an American, despite almost half a century in France. She connected her role as

LEFT: During the Occupation, Gertrude and Alice grew most of their food in their garden. Villagers conspired to keep their presence in the French countryside a secret from the Germans.

America is my country and Paris is my home town and it is as it has come to be.

literary innovator and cultural pioneer to being a Californian with an intrinsic affinity for the new. She has been called "the voice of American common sense, American pragmatism, America living in the present."[31]

Despite her sweeping and often offensive generalizations about various national and racial characteristics, her writings on America and Americans are usually poignant and apt. Being an American in France was the experience that both made it possible for her to write and was what she often wrote about.

Gertrude Stein and Alice B. Toklas were fiercely American, but in thirty years, they returned to their native shores just once, in 1934, for the lecture tour Gertrude made following the overnight success of *The Autobiography of Alice B. Toklas*. The publication of the immensely readable, entertaining "autobiography" was the turning point in Gertrude's life: at 58 she received her first book contract and the recognition as a writer for which she had worked for so long. The book was reprinted for the Book-of-the-Month Club, and many predicted a Pulitzer prize.

America treated Gertrude Stein's tour as the return of its prodigal daughter. Her ship was met by newsreel cameramen and journalists of every hue. *The Saturday Review of Literature* ran a banner headline: "Exile's Return"; the *New York Post* reported, rather unpleasantly: "That grand old expatriate ... returned to these shores today after thirty-one cloistered years in Paris. She brought with her Alice B. Toklas, her queer, birdlike shadow .... her girl Friday talked about Miss Stein, when she talked at all." Other newspapers debated whether Alice Toklas actually existed, or whether it was she who really called the shots in their relationship.

Of course, the press made plenty of jokes about Gertrude's writing, and most journalists could not resist a few paragraphs in parody of her repetitive style. *The Detroit News* announced that "A New York literary analyst professes to understand the poems of Gertrude Stein. It complicates the matter considerably, as we must now try to understand the analyst." Less humorously, the *Journal of the American Medical Association* ran an article by B.F. Skinner, which analyzed Gertrude's writing for indications of mental disorder.

LEFT: An American in France.

N.Y. World - Telegram · Oct 25. 54

Alice Toklas Hides in Shadows of Stein

Mouselike Companion Does Not Show Exotic Air Author Claims for Her.

By EVELYN SEELEY.

EVERYBODY knows Gertrude Stein and her brilliant wit and esoteric writings. Everyone has argued over her these many years. But almost nobody knows Alice B. Toklas, her indispensable and willing shadow, and some even doubt she exists.

Someone Called Stein Sails With Alice B. Toklas

Bon Voyage Party Presents New Slant on Question of Who's No. 1 of That Pair

Secretary Rules Roost

Employer Has a Hard Time Getting Word in Edgewise!

Alice B. Toklas, product of San

ABOVE: The media are fascinated by, but just can't figure out, the relationship between Gertrude and Alice.

Despite such insults, Gertrude thoroughly enjoyed her trip around America, most of which she had never seen before. She sent a card to Janet Flanner, postmarked February 1935, "My dear Janet, Yes we are having a good time a really good time and it is very exciting and very natural and we like it a lot, and do not pine [?] at all for Paris, certainly I liked having your letter lots of love Gtde."

Gertrude also loved the sudden fame and fortune. She bought a new car and a Hermes coat for her dog Basket.

And suddenly she was receiving unsolicited letters from publishers; this one came from Scribner's: "Dear Miss Stein ... I am interested to hear that you are working on a novel; you must naturally realize that we should always be interested in anything you do."

Ironically, it was not her painstakingly developed literary innovations that brought Gertrude before the reading public. The book that catapulted her to fame was not even written in her own enigmatic repetitive style, but rather adopted the ordinary, direct speaking voice of Alice B. Toklas. Alice, of course, denied that she played any role other than typist: "Oh no. What could I contribute?"[32] Yet Virgil Thomson, who knew them both well, claims that:

> This book is in every way except actual authorship Alice
> Toklas's book; it reflects her mind, her language, her private

ABOVE: "Coming back to the United States after 31 years everything seizes my interest and seizes it hard. The buildings in the air and the people in the street, they're all exciting." — Gertrude Stein, interviewed at Columbia University on NBC radio, 12 November 1934.

view of Gertrude, also her unique narrative powers. Every story in it is told as Alice herself had always told it.[33]

If this is true, then privately Gertrude's success must have been bittersweet. Gertrude, obsessed with the question of her own identity, became famous for writing in someone else's voice. As Katherine Anne Porter put it: "She had never learned who she was, and yet suddenly she had become somebody else."[34]

She was also somebody else because fame changed her. It had to. As she wrote in *Everybody's Autobiography*,

> ... suddenly it was all different, what I did had a value that
> made people ready to pay, up to that time everything had a
> value because nobody was ready to pay. It is funny about
> money. And it is funny about identity. You are you because
> your little dog knows you, but when your public knows you
> and does not want to pay for you and when your public knows
> you and does want to pay for you, you are not the same you.

36, RUE BONAPARTE - PARIS VIˣ

December Tenth

dear Gertrude, I'm glad I refused to do a Profile of you for
The NewYorker —my reason was excellent; I said since I couldn't
write about you better than you'd written about yourself in
Autobiography, I felt it was improper to write at all - for
if I'd written it and it had been added to everything else
they've written and pictured about and around you, the name
                                              The
of the magazine would have to be changed from/NewYorker
   The   The
to/Gertruder.   Or maybe/Gertrudest. Are you and Miss Toklas
have a good or a bad time, or a mixture, or nothing of either
enough to be sure until later? Why don't you both run for
President while you're out there, you could get the job easy.
Friends in New York sent me the boat interviews, one of which
seemed to me excellent, intelligent. You seem to me to make
                                                       can
such sense in what you say I can't see how anybody find it
                              but
cryptic or anger-making; I think maybe I'm 42 and know that,
as a beginning of knowledge:
though; maybe when I was 32 I didn't know what you meant
either.   This is to thank you for sending me the Autobiography
in French and to wish you and Miss T a Merry Christmas and
                                       Your tour is too
to tell you I think you're both superb. It's an ordeal by
soda-pop which burns and is licquid but is neither fire nor
water; you've both come through immortally.

                    Love and greetings,

                              Janet F

It was not whether she wrote as Gertrude or as Alice, or even how she wrote at all; it was the fascinating friendships she wrote about which placed the book at the top of the bestseller lists. *The Autobiography of Alice B. Toklas* chronicles these famous friendships—and was to be responsible for ending many of them.

While Gertrude and Alice were touring their homeland, trouble was brewing in their hometown. *The Autobiography* produced a storm of protest, mostly by those depicted in its pages. The anger was so great that *transition* magazine, edited by Eugene Jolas, published a supplementary issue titled "Testimony against Gertrude Stein" solely to allow the "injured parties" to "correct what was said about them."

Lurking behind some of these "corrections" seem to be deeper, private angers, and perhaps resentment over her newfound fame. For example, Matisse wrote, "With regard to the purchase of the Cézanne [which Gertrude had incorrectly described]: there was no tent in the picture, it was a Cézanne with three women bathers and several trees …" He charged Gertrude with deliberately writing this falsehood about the painting.

Braque has a more legitimate claim. He was understandably upset because Gertrude wrote that Picasso had invented Cubism, whereas Braque felt he and Picasso were engaged in a joint "search for the anonymous personality …" Clearly Gertrude's version made Braque's personality too anonymous for his liking.

The famous falling-out between Hemingway and Gertrude Stein also involved a bruised male ego. In *The Autobiography,* Gertrude claimed that Hemingway was a great pupil of hers: "He copied the manuscript of *The Making of Americans* and corrected the proof … In correcting these proofs Hemingway learned a great deal and he admired all that he learned."

Hemingway, after Gertrude's death, tried to set the record straight in his "Letter of Exceptional Literary Importance." He couldn't totally refute that she had been his mentor, but suggested that theirs was a more reciprocal relationship:

LEFT: Janet Flanner seems to have been as overwhelmed by Gertrude and Alice's American tour as they themselves were.

65

Testimony
against
Gertrude Stein

February 1935

Georges Braque

Eugene Jolas

Maria Jolas

Henri Matisse

André Salmon

Tristan Tzara

Servire Press
The Hague

I always loved her very much ... She had, or Alice had, a sort of necessity to break off friendships and she only gave real loyalty to people who were inferior to her. She had to attack me because she learned to write dialogue from me just as I learned the wonderful rhythms in prose from her ...

Janet Flanner never found traces of Hemingway's style in Gertrude Stein's dialogue, but noticed that "her rhythms emerged in the style of Ernest Hemingway ... He and Sherwood Anderson were the two people who were most affected, most influenced by, the quietude of her speech and felt that in the rhythm of the repetitions in her writing they arrived at their own styles."[35]

Writing is a solitary venture. Hemingway, Sherwood Anderson, Scott Fitzgerald, and many others learned from Gertrude Stein but, as Hemingway rightly points out, "Then you have to do it alone and by yourself and keep on learning; only you are alone ..." Nonetheless, it is not difficult to imagine how Gertrude must have felt as she watched her "protégés" go on to greater critical and popular acclaim while she remained ridiculed and unpublished for so long. They must have loved her constant dismissals of their success: "... if the outside [world] puts a value on you then all your inside gets to be outside. I used to tell all the men who were being successful young how bad this was for them ..."[36]

Publicly Gertrude always denied harboring hard feelings. When a publisher told her, "We want the comprehensible thing, the thing the public can understand," she answered with, "My work would have been no use to anyone if the public had understood me early and first."[37] She put up a tough front:

I found the money to publish [*Three Lives,* her first book] myself. No publisher would look at it. But that did not discourage me; I was not the first author who paid his own admission... Lack of popular success ... is the last of my worries. I am working for what will endure, not for a public.

LEFT: After the publication of *The Autobiography of Alice B. Toklas,* some of Gertrude Stein's former friends set out to establish that she was not "in any way concerned with the shaping of the epoch she attempts to describe" and that "she had no understanding of what really was happening around her."

Once you have a public you are never free.... The early set-backs aid the eventual greatness. Quick success is killing.[38]

But it was the lack of success, year after year, which was killing. Throughout her many unpublished decades the negative responses did bother Gertrude enormously. Privately she wrote in 1913, "it's getting anything at all printed thats my worry." Three years later she wrote, "Get kind of sad and restless every now and then because I can't be published. Would love to be published." Often when sending her manuscripts to editors, she'd anticipate the rejection and ask them to read the submissions several times before deciding. She confided to a friend, "I do so love to be printed. Even the war has not made me less fond of that."

Over thirty years later, on her deathbed, Gertrude made her last request: that all her many unpublished manuscripts see their way into print. Alice was to outlive her by over twenty years, until that enormous task was accomplished and she could join Gertrude in Père Lachaise cemetery in Paris.

In those lonely decades, Alice wrote several books of her own, including her memoirs, *What is Remembered.* It might well have been titled *What is Forgotten* for, according to Alice, "I could have begun with the beginning and given you everything connected with every day along the line. Until Gertrude died. I lost my memory then, because I think I was upset and my head, when it came back, just wasn't clear."[39] If Gertrude is best known for what she wrote with Alice's "unique narrative powers" and in Alice's persona, Alice ends her own life story with Gertrude's death and in Gertrude's famous last words: "What is the answer? I was silent. In that case, she said, what is the question?"

3

AMAZONES ET SIRÈNES

"As an Amazon, Miss Barney was not belligerent. On the contrary, she was charming, and all dressed in white with her blond coloring, most attractive. Many of her sex found her fatally so ..."

—Sylvia Beach, *Shakespeare and Company*

By 1972, the year she died in Paris at the age of 95, Natalie Clifford Barney had long been a legendary figure in France. She had written countless poems and 13 books, been immortalized by other writers in at least half-a-dozen works of fiction and in numerous memoirs, and had hosted an international salon for many of the leading writers, artists, and intellectuals of this century. But none of this was the reason for her legendary status.

Rather, she was what her biographer George Wickes has aptly called "unquestionably the leading lesbian of her time."[1] She devoted her life to praising the joys of, and indeed promoting an ethos of, lesbianism.

Natalie surrounded herself with a coterie of beautiful women, virtually all of whom were former, present or future lovers. While in her twenties, she and the poet Renée Vivien travelled to Lesbos to set up a lesbian school for poetry and love (the scheme was curtailed when Renée's other lover, a wealthy Dutch baroness, hauled her back to France). The qualities of Sappho that Natalie admired—a love of beauty and sensuality, the freedom to love without jealousy or moral judgment—were signposts by which she set out to live her own life. Although her plans for Lesbos were stymied, Natalie gathered a similar

ABOVE: "Our understanding natures coincided, completing one another" — Natalie Barney left, on her relationship with Romaine Brooks.

community of women around her in Paris, and held pagan rituals in her garden.

Usually these theatrical events were attended only by women, but one afternoon when Colette performed, André Germain was on hand to record it for posterity. In his book about Proust, Germain devoted a chapter to the literary women of the era which he titled "Amazones et Sirènes" (In *Remembrance of Things Past*, Proust had titled *his* chapter on these women "Sodom and Gomorrah"). Germain recalled:

> Several years later I was to see Colette again, naked this time
> and imitating a faun. It was in a garden which belonged to a
> friend whose every wish I then obeyed, Nathalie [sic] Clifford
> Barney … Nathalie had summoned me for a ceremony in
> honor of a poetess whom I had not known but pursued
> beyond the grave, Renée Vivien. The poems murmured and at
> the end sobbed by that unfortunate young woman [Renée]
> struck me and charmed me, despite their pagan audacity …[2]

In a recent study of the work of both Renée Vivien and Natalie Barney, Karla Jay has attempted to restore Natalie Barney's reputation as a poet which has been eclipsed by the notoriety she has achieved

ABOVE: Natalie held pagan rituals and "theatricals" for women in her garden. Participants included Colette, Sarah Bernhardt, and Eva Palmer. This one was exceptional in allowing men and boys to assume leading roles.

as a seductress of women. Alas, Jay found in the end that her literary achievements amounted to many but not much. Her calling as a poet could never match her calling as a lover, despite her pursuit of a lesbian aesthetic in which poetry and love were inseparable. There are moments of brilliance in her writings, yet her far greater literary contribution rested in identifying and promoting the creative genius of others. Her wide capacity for love nourished and supported a century of female creativity, not only her own but that of her innumerable lovers and intimate friends. Her art was that of love, and she was a prolific artist, much to the chagrin of her jealous lifelong partner, the painter Romaine Brooks.

Natalie and Romaine were both enormously wealthy American expatriates in Paris, but here their similarities ended. Romaine wrote to Natalie after half a century together:

[I'm] thinking about our long friendship which on my part is as great as ever; of our natures that differ fundamentally: you needing people as fuel for producing the sparks that animate your rare gift of rapid words and I needing solitude for creating … my world of art …

Poet Renée Vivien with Natalie — they
~~~ed reviving the golden age of Sappho.

Romaine's calm, powerful self-portrait,
~ in 1923 when she was 49.

But Natalie believed that their fundamentally different natures complemented each other and enabled their relationship to endure where others burnt themselves out. From Renée Vivien to Djuna Barnes to Dolly Wilde (Natalie's lover of ten years), Natalie Barney was repeatedly drawn to extraordinarily gifted women who were bent on self-destruction. Of Djuna Barnes, Natalie wrote: "A rough diamond sort of genius who cut everything to pieces and then blamed the cuts." In her memoirs, she reflected on why her relationship with Romaine broke from this pattern, and how the relationship kept Romaine from joining the ranks of the "self-destroyers":

They were a wild, bacchanalian lot … and although I sympathized with them, I could not suffer their fate. Had I not ridden wild horses myself and been carried away, but they had not thrown me nor had I risen to such heights, perhaps because I had neither their gifts nor their guts. But Romaine who had both, had hewn her way through equally adverse circumstances and soberly braved hardships surpassing theirs and come out on top with her all-dominating art … putting her soul into everything she believed in or loved or undertook. The intensity with which … would make such a pursuit unbearable had not our understanding natures coincided, completing one another.

The Allure of Paris

Natalie and Romaine were the first among the community of American expatriate women to arrive in Paris; both came intermittently in the 1890s and Natalie returned to settle in Paris in 1902. "This wild girl from Cincinnati" as Natalie was dubbed, was not only a very rich heiress, but also incredibly appealing. On a visit to France with her family in 1899, she had, at 22, seduced one of the most sensuous

73

and famous Parisian courtesans of *la belle époque,* Liane de Pougy. In *Idylle saphique,* a novel which rocked the social world of upper-class Paris on its publication in 1901, Liane de Pougy had written an explicit, thinly-veiled account of this affair—the first of many works of fiction inspired by Natalie (two years later she made an appearance in one of Colette's *Claudine* books). Natalie's father hauled her back to Washington where her family was then living and, futilely, selected an eligible fiancé from her many male suitors.

Natalie, too, celebrated the notorious love affair in *Lettres à une connue,* which her publisher decided was too scandalous to print, and in *Quelques Portraits—Sonnets de Femmes,* 34 love poems to women. Illustrated by her mother—who had not known exactly how the illustrations would be used—the slender volume created a scandal in Washington. Newspaper headlines read "Sappho in Washington"—but it was her being "in Washington" and not being a "Sappho," which disturbed Natalie. She was already beyond needing society's approval:

> I considered myself without shame: albinos aren't reproached for having pink eyes and whitish hair, why should they hold it against me for being a lesbian? It's a question of nature: my queerness isn't a vice, isn't "deliberate," and harms no one. What do I care, afterall, if they vilify or judge me according to their prejudices?

ABOVE: Romaine painted Natalie as "L'Amazone" in 1920.

Fortunately her mother was sympathetic to Natalie's frustrations. A painter who had studied with Whistler in Paris, Alice Pike Barney took her daughter away from the dull, stifling, upper-class Washington society that Natalie so disliked and returned to the Paris they both loved. To Natalie, "Paris has always seemed ... the only city where you can live and express yourself as you please."[3]

Of all the American expatriate women in Paris, Natalie seems to have brought the lightest cultural baggage, and certainly none of the

ABOVE: This "wild girl from Cincinnati" took Paris by storm.

American Protestant morality, with her to France. She was equally at home in English and French, both of which she spoke in an antiquated nineteenth-century style. She privately published her volumes of lesbian love poems in classic French romantic style, but moved rather carelessly between one literary form and another in her poetry, epigrams, novels, plays, memoirs, and autobiographical texts. She prioritized living over writing, saying that, "My life is my work, my writings are but the result."[4]

Natalie Barney's epigrams, or pensées, as she called them, can be seen as capsules of feminist logic, turning around masculine assumptions with feminine wit in much the way Oscar Wilde turned around heterosexual assumptions with homosexual wit. In her *Pensées d'une amazone* she wrote about the masculinity of war and its futility; the ridiculousness of men and the oppression of women:

> If love existed among men, they would have already found the means of proving it.

> Man, that incompletely weaned creature …

ABOVE: Natalie Barney, as Remy de Gaurmont's L'Amazone.

If maternity worked backwards, beginning with the pains of childbirth, there would still be mothers, but they would be willing heroines, not victims of a mistake or wretched martyrs of one of nature's tricks.

The Frenchman is, in fact, absentminded; he has submitted to the war; he has equally submitted to victory, and will not even condescend to profit from it.

Romaine Brooks: Working Out Life Through Art

For Romaine Brooks, in direct contrast to Natalie Barney, her work was her life. In her work she exorcised the demons of her childhood—an insane brother and a cruel, unloving mother—a time so awful that those who read her unpublished memoirs refused to believe them. Romaine arrived in Paris by way of Rome, Capri, London and St. Ives, after a brief marriage to a homosexual man, an unwanted child given up for adoption, a serious bout of pneumonia, and several unsatisfactory love affairs. After this long and difficult journey, Romaine was homeless and restless. She found serenity only in her work. For fifteen years she painted in obscurity, isolation, and poverty (her great wealth came suddenly, upon her mother's death). As the first and only woman student in the Art Academy in Rome, she had suffered humiliating harassment and ridicule as well as near-starvation.

Not at all gregarious by nature, Romaine's acquaintances were mainly people she met through Natalie, and most of these she didn't like. But she befriended one shy artist who was to become a close friend: the Irish-born designer and architect, Eileen Gray. Eileen had moved to Paris in 1902, to be in the company of independent, creative women. Her participation in the 1913 *Salon des Artistes Décorateurs* brought her sparse, Modernist designs to the attention of art collector Jacques Doucet, her first patron, and earned her critical acclaim.

Similarly, Romaine's first exhibition, in Galeries Durand-Ruel in 1910, was a big success—but, sadly, it could also be seen as the peak of her career. Although influenced to some extent by the Symbolists, Romaine's work pays no notice to the far more significant art movement of the nineteenth century, Impressionism. Unlike Eileen Gray, who was influenced by the geometry of Cubism and of the Dutch De

Stijl group, Romaine did not care for artistic trends and painted as though the twentieth century and its many artistic shake-ups were not occurring around her. As time went on, she was increasingly discredited for being outmoded and out of touch—as though she were a journalist who didn't bother to read the newspaper, rather than a painter guided by her own mind's eye.

The Salon, Out of Time

Natalie Barney also seemed to exist outside of time. She is now viewed as embodying the contradictions of the *belle époque,* a period caught in the tension of looking forward to the new century while clinging reluctantly to the old. But her contemporary Marguerite Yourcenar disagreed, saying to her when Natalie was already in her nineties: "Really, the eighteenth century is your time, much more than la Belle Époque. How young you are, Natalie, for a contemporary of Madame du Deffand and Rivarol."[5] Although snubbed by the more staid members of upper-class French society because of her sexual notoriety, in fashion, politics, and resistance to anything new, Natalie was as old-fashioned and conservative as they.

She flouted social convention in certain circles, but she craved social acceptance in others. When her young lover Renée Vivien died of anorexia, alcoholism, and a broken heart, Natalie sent her poems about Renée to the leading man of letters in France. Remy de Gaurmont was at once the editor of the influential *Mercure de France,* a prolific poet, essayist and novelist, literary critic of the Symbolist movement, and mentor to, among others, T.S. Eliot and Ezra Pound. Despite a disfiguring disease which kept him in seclusion, he befriended Natalie and published elegant essays in *Mercure de France* addressed to a mysterious Amazon. The consequence of his unrequited love for Natalie Barney in his dying years was that she achieved an artistic and social prominence she could never have gained otherwise, and which she desperately needed to fulfill her social ambitions. In 1909, she established

RIGHT: One of the salon regulars was Germaine Beaumont, short-term lover and long-term friend of Natalie Barney's, whom after forty years she still called "My Natalie." As Solita Solano indicated on this photograph, she was the protégée of Colette, but also was a highly regarded writer in her own right.

Colette's
protégée

a salon in her Left Bank house that would continue for 60 years and encompass many French, American and English artists, writers and celebrities including André Gide, Jean Cocteau, Paul Valéry, Colette, Ezra Pound, Gertrude Stein, Edith Sitwell, Ford Madox Ford, Sherwood Anderson, Marie Laurencin, Thornton Wilder, Janet Flanner, Gabriele D'Annunzio, Edna St. Vincent Millay, Isadora Duncan, Rainer Maria Rilke, and Djuna Barnes.

According to Solita Solano, journalist and friend of Janet Flanner, "Natalie did not collect modern art; she collected people, and you could be sure of being dazzled any Friday (her day) you dropped in for tea."[6] On one particularly dazzling Friday Greta Garbo showed up, brought by her lover Mercedes D'Acosta. Garbo created quite a stir, according to Truman Capote, as Natalie and her friends "thought of Garbo as the *ne plus ultra* of what they were all about."[7]

For 45 of those 60 years, Natalie Barney was dutifully served by her housekeeper Berthe Cleyrergue. Janet Flanner has called Berthe "so loyal, she practically took on Natalie's taste," whereas Natalie called her "my librarian, manager, receptionist, nurse, handyman, cook, chambermaid, and confidence man, companion of my winters and of all the troubles that she helps me to iron out …"[8] Berthe knew most of the salon guests and the gossip surrounding them (exchanging it with a select few at the door before they came in), if not the literature for which they were renowned. She describes the salon:

> It was the literary salon itself. There were literary — poetry conversations, about which book had just come out. It was young people coming with their manuscripts. So there was Madame Radelais, Janet Flanner, Germaine Beaumont, who would take the manuscripts and eight or ten days later, or a fortnight later, bring them back to tell this young man or woman, if it was any good. And then, they would be recommended to a publisher. Gertrude Stein used to come; there were a lot of people. Colette was a great friend. In 1928, together with Miss Romaine Brooks, Colette was a friend to Miss Barney, the very best of her friends all her life, for 62 years. Miss Barney would always say this to me, so, if she said it, I can repeat it.[9]

Colette in Literature and Love

Janet Flanner has confirmed that Colette, regardless of her three husbands and several female lovers, was, after Romaine Brooks and Lily de Clermont-Tonnerre, one of the great loves of Natalie's life:

> [Natalie] was intimate with Colette … Colette must have been more satisfactory than almost anyone else in her life. Then there were the younger women, whom it would not be fair to name, since they were people with whom Natalie merely fell in love …[10]

One of France's most celebrated and esteemed authors, Colette immortalized the lesbian society of Paris in her *The Pure and the Impure,* which Colette considered to be her best book. The shocked and offended readers of a Paris weekly, *Gringoire,* in which it was serialized in 1930, disagreed: after its fourth installment the editor, bowing to his readership, discontinued the serialization so abruptly that, according to Janet Flanner, "the word FIN, The End, appears in the middle of a sentence that is never completed."[11]

In her introduction to an English translation of *The Pure and the Impure,* Janet Flanner wrote that she could "think of no other female writer endowed with this double [male and female] comprehension whereby she understood and accepted the naturalness of sex wherever found or however fragmented and reapportioned."[12] Perhaps Colette's ability to live in male and female, heterosexual and homosexual, worlds all at once gave her this double comprehension. Natalie Barney, however, had another view of Colette's serial marriages: she wrote in her 1929 book, *Adventures of the Mind,* that Colette loved, among other things, "having one man at a time in order to keep her in slavery."

Colette was on her third (and last) husband by the time she wrote *The Pure and the Impure;* she had come a long way from being a bawdy music hall performer to earning France's highest award, the Legion of Honor. She could now afford to be the cool, detached observer of the sexual escapades of her youth, whereas in her early autobiographical novels, she had written from the midst of her tumultuous and disreputable life, motivated by passion and revenge.

ABOVE: "Colette seemed to have a hermaphroditic duality in her understanding and twofold loyalties," according to Janet Flanner.

When Colette first married the theatre editor, Parisian wit and general man-about-town known as Willy, she was just a country girl of nineteen and he considerably older and already established. By then he had an entire literary factory on the go, hiring ghostwriters by the dozens. He added Colette to their numbers, and locked her in a room to write her schoolgirl memoirs to which, like everything else, he put his own name. But, she wondered, what choice did she have? "It was marry Willy or become an old maid or a teacher."[13]

What Willy didn't expect was the overnight sensation *Claudine à l'école* created. This led to a demand for Claudine sequels and plays that only Colette herself could fulfill. Decades later, when her name had been restored to the title page, she still credited Willy, not as author, nor even literary collaborator, as he liked to imagine himself, but for getting her work published in the first place:

> When I had finished, I handed over to my husband a closely-written manuscript … He skimmed through it and said: "I made a mistake, this can't be of the slightest use …" Released, I went back to the sofa, to the cat, to books … The exercise books remained for two years at the bottom of a drawer. One day Willy decided to tidy up the contents of his desk.
>
> "Fancy," said Monsieur Willy. "I thought I had put them in the waste-paper basket." He opened one exercise book and turned over the pages … He swept up the exercise-books haphazard, pounced on his flat-brimmed hat and rushed off to a publisher … And that was how I became a writer.
>
> But that was also how I very nearly missed becoming a writer. I lacked the literary vocation and it is probable that I should never have produced another line if, after the success of *Claudine à l'école*, other imposed tasks had not, little by little, gotten me into the habit of writing.[14]

Although one of France's greatest writers, Colette always doubted her literary skills and her right to claim a "literary vocation." She felt it was only strenuous self-discipline, rather than talent, that enabled her to write: "If I were to relax the merciless control I inflict on my prose, I know well that I would soon cease to be the anxious and diligent prose writer that I am and become nothing more than bad poet."[15]

After their messy divorce, in which Willy tried to claim all future revenue from Colette's writings published under his name, Willy wrote that the marriage had been the only respectable solution to Colette's scandalous behavior. In one of his later novels he portrays her "as an intelligent and sly country girl, poor as a churchmouse, who cannot marry in her own village because of a fugue with a music teacher." Although Willy's was a piece of fiction, Colette disputed the facts: the piano teacher was a woman, in Paris, and she and Willy were already married.

In her own early fictions Colette stuck so closely to the facts that she barely paused to alter the names of her schoolmates in the *Claudine* series, causing them tremendous embarrassment and lifelong hostility towards her. Janet Flanner, in her introduction to *The Pure and the Impure,* described what she called Colette's "favorite writing formula" as "autobiographic novelizing" and went on to easily decode the characters. Of the character "La Chevalière" whose "real title was too weighty to be mentioned" Janet Flanner wrote:

> Stripped of all the fictitious trappings with which Colette loyally sought to disguise her, she was easily recognizable to Parisians as the ex-Marquise de Belboeuf, with whom Colette had lived for six years after the end of her first marriage … She looked like a distinguished, refined, no-longer-young man, for she always wore men's clothes, indeed wore quite a lot of them, which made her look plump [to] hide what might have seemed her effeminate figure … She was addressed as Monsieur le Marquis.[16]

The infamous couple created a scandal virtually everywhere they went. They performed together in music hall pantomimes throughout France, with the ex-Marquise, known as "Missy," playing the male role. Reviewing Colette's performance in a pantomime in 1906, a critic called on Lesbos to imply that Colette was playing to the women rather than the men in the audience: "She struck some ceremonial poses, during which her skirt rose still higher, and the Mytilène elite became delirious." At the Moulin Rouge, the sold-out, black-tie opening crowd was so scandalized by the near-nudity, female crossdressing, and, above all, by the kiss between Colette and Missy that it turned into a screaming, fighting mob; the show was shut down by the police.

On the domestic front, however, Missy and Colette settled into

le pied de nez

ABOVE: When Missy and Colette performed a music hall pantomime at the Moulin Rouge, the police shut down the show.

peaceful bliss. Colette's mother, who closely followed in the press the unconventional behavior of her daughter, was relieved that after the disastrous marriage to Willy, "you have with you someone who loves you truly." Janet Flanner recalled that this domesticity centered around good food: "Her household always included an excellent devoted cook for Colette was a gourmet and a good cook herself …"[17] But it was precisely her cooking for which Colette apologized:

[Undated] Dearest Janet

How kind of you. This poor lunch I gave you, which gave me the pleasure of your company only deserved that you would say: My girl you are not much of a hausfrau. And I'll remember your quiche lorraine as a remarkable peace [sic] of cement … When do I take you to a decent dinner?[18]

The arrangement between Missy and Colette, seemingly modeled on heterosexual marriage, and Missy's notorious cross-dressing, are matters Colette has her characters take up in *The Pure and the Impure*:

> "... a couple of women can live together a long time and be happy. But if one of the two women lets herself behave in the slightest like what I call a pseudo-man, then ..."
>
> "Then the couple become unhappy?"
>
> "... You see, when a woman remains a woman, she is a complete human being. She lacks nothing, even as far as her *amie* is concerned. But if she ever gets it into her head to try to be a man, then she's grotesque. What is more ridiculous, what is sadder, than a woman pretending to be a man? On that subject, you'll never get me to change my mind. La Luciènne, from the time she adopted men's clothes, well! ... Do you imagine her life wasn't poisoned from then on?"
>
> "Poisoned by what?"

Many of the "female figures in this transvestite society of the 'Pure and the Impure,'" as Janet Flanner called them, were modelled on women who attended Natalie's weekly salon.

Truman Capote commented that the salon was fascinating for its literary connections as well as its sexual intrigue:

> Miss Barney's circle was not limited to lesbians . . She had *tout Paris.* Many of them were friends of Proust who had been characters in *Remembrance of Things Past*—like the Duchesse de Clermont-Tonnerre. Miss Barney would say to me very specifically that she wanted me to meet somebody because that person was so-and-so in Proust.[19]

The Adverse Sexes: War and Feminism

The Duchesse de Clermont-Tonnerre, whose aristocratic family went as far back as Henry IV, was by no means as stuffy as her name. Financially ruined by divorce and then by war, she earned her own way as a writer, volunteered in a military hospital during the First World War, and, in numerous radical newspaper editorials and public lectures, advocated communism, for which she earned the nickname,

A OVE: Romaine Brooks circa 1935

"The Red Duchess." Natalie had to bail her out financially on occasion. Although politically at odds with each other, Lily de Clermont-Tonnerre was Natalie's Great Love during the Great War, and the reason Natalie could not tear herself away from France, even after she had packed and shipped her belongings back to the United States. In her memoirs she recalled Lily's plea:

> On the first of August [1914] in Paris, my French friend [Lily] asked: "You are not going back to America, are you?"
>
> "My family is awaiting me there, my trunks and my papers have already left for Le Havre."
>
> "But you, you were with us in peace, you won't leave us now there is to be war?"

Lily prevailed; ironically, had she not, Natalie would never have met Romaine during those years, although later neither could remember which year it was. From the start Romaine had to share Natalie with Lily de Clermont-Tonnerre, as she would have to do with all of Natalie's other lovers for the next half a century. But she admired and respected Lily, unlike most of Natalie's subsequent liaisons. It was Lily who introduced Romaine to Eileen Gray; Eileen had worked as an ambulance driver under Lily's supervision during the First World War.

Romaine had great respect for women war workers generally, and painted her powerful "La France Croisée" whose face, recalling that of the dancer Ida Rubenstein, Romaine's previous lover, shows the strength and calm with which women met the horrors of war. The painting inspired four poems by Gabriele D'Annunzio, with whom Romaine also had had a tortured love affair. The poems, together with a reproduction of her painting, were published as a booklet to raise money for the Red Cross.

The poet Lucie Delarue Mardrus, a close friend of Colette's, also volunteered as a nurse during the war.

She was married to Dr. Joseph-Charles Mardrus (whom Natalie always called Dr. Jesus-Christ Mardrus), famous for his translation of *The Arabian Nights* into French. Nicknamed "Archangel Amazon," Lucie Delarue Mardrus was another lover of Natalie Barney's and wrote about their love in overtly erotic poetry (posthumously published by Natalie as *Nos secrètes amours)* and a play, *Sapho désesperée.*

Her husband had endured the affair for two years, but now that he was completing the sixteenth and final volume of *The Arabian Nights*, he turned his attentions back to his wife and promptly carried her off to Africa.

Lucie later portrayed Natalie in an unflattering—indeed, devastating—light in her 1930 novel, *L'Ange et les Pervers*, where her character heartlessly plays with her lovers' emotions.

> For you are terribly American, for all your cosmopolitan airs. You make twenty-five rendezvous all over Paris for the same hour ... You have the restless disease which comes from being dragged around ocean liners, trains, and hotels while too young, like all little Yankees who are too rich ...
>
> You invent little situations, you play childish games with love. At bottom you are a bunch of schoolgirls—dangerous schoolgirls at that—for in the midst of all this there is a man who loved his wife and who has lost her, a woman who was leading a peaceful life and who is now launched on adventures that lead her astray.

Harsh words, but after their tumultuous affair, Lucie and Natalie settled into a lifelong friendship, and Lucie divorced "Jesus-Christ."

Despite the decision of her many friends, including fellow Americans Sylvia Beach, Gertrude Stein, and Alice B. Toklas, to enlist in the war effort, Natalie wanted no part of the "ambulance aids" brigade, as she sarcastically referred to them. Natalie felt that war was a logical extension of ordinary male aggression, of which women were the innocent victims. Her *Pensées d'une amazone* opens with a section which gives pithy expression to these theories, entitled "The Adverse Sexes: War and Feminism." While her friends were facing the daily horrors of military hospitals, Natalie was organizing a congress of female pacifists. The meetings were held in Natalie's Temple of Friendship, a small, four-columned Doric temple built in a corner of the wild, spacious garden hidden away in the courtyard at 20 rue Jacob. Some women claimed these pacifist meetings were the only place where it was safe to express any fear or hatred of war, which did nothing to bring peace but somehow made them feel better.

Although her political views were conservative, bordering on the fascist, anti-Semitic, and outright bizarre as she got older, Natalie

Barney was in some ways her own brand of devout feminist, espousing a feminism which did not extend to all womankind, despite her claim that "we endeavored to include women of all classes, professions and all countries" in the pacifist meetings held in her temple. Nor was she much concerned with women's entry into politics and other male dominated fields, although she would have been pleased if women took over the business of running society altogether. In her memoirs she wrote:

> With or without [women's] rights everything seems to be going
> on much as before their voting and never was their influence
> more needed—and lacking … If the voices of women are
> hushed up like children's—they the courageous mothers of men
> —if they have no worthy representatives of their cause, if they
> cannot rule equally with men over the lives together created,
> should not the stronger in the instinct of race preservations
> prevail; and the Matriarchal again dominate the Patriarchal?

The most practical application of her feminist ideals could be found in her devotion to encouraging, advocating, and even financing women's literary and artistic endeavors. Although not known for her generosity, she used some of her seemingly infinite funds to publish privately women writers, to award a "Renée Vivien Prize" and to support those, such as Djuna Barnes, who fell on hard times. Natalie's Académie des Femmes was her answer to the Académie Française, that venerable but blinkered institution that excluded women. Colette had been promoted to the highest position permitted a woman within the Legion of Honor, but still could not be elected to the Académie Française on account of her gender; she was of course a founding member of Natalie's Académie. Although many men, from Rainer Maria Rilke to Ezra Pound (with whom she would play tennis in the 1920s) attended Natalie's salon, the special Académie des Femmes gatherings would always be dedicated to honoring a woman writer and would at times be open to women only.

Among the women honored by the Académie were Djuna Barnes,

RIGHT: "La France Croisée" by Romaine Brooks, 1914. Romaine's portrait of a Red Cross nurse as a symbol for France at war.

Edna St. Vincent Millay, and Gertrude Stein, and it was here that Colette performed a selection from her play *La Vagabonde* in 1922.

A Clash of Centuries: Natalie Barney and Gertrude Stein

In her own, informal way, Natalie probably did more than anyone, aside from Sylvia Beach and Adrienne Monnier, to bridge French and expatriate literary communities in Paris. In 1926 she wrote to Gertrude Stein,

ABOVE: A drawing of the temple in Natalie's garden. As if expecting Natalie Barney to live at this address someday, the temple had been inscribed with the words "à l'amitié"—"to friendship."

> The other night "au Caméléon" I realized how little the French "femmes de lettres" know of the English and Americans and vice versa … I wish I might bring about a better "entente," and hope therefore to organize here this winter, and this spring, readings and presentations that will enable our mind-allies to appreciate each other … Colette has promised to act a scene from her "Vagabonde" which is to appear later in a theatre in Paris—I should like to add at least one anglo-saxon to this first group, and thought that you, presented by yourself would make a good representation—and balance the French trio. Will you! Shall we? … Hoping my "petit projet" may meet with your approval and receive your participation. With affectionate greetings to you and your friend, in which Romaine Brooks joins me -

It is hard to imagine that Natalie Barney, with her nineteenth- (or even eighteenth-) century style and her flamboyant lesbian sexuality, and Gertrude Stein, with her avant-garde literary style and her traditional "companionship" with Alice B. Toklas, had much in common. Most commentary about Gertrude Stein denies altogether the importance of women in her life aside from Alice, and characterizes her as "male identified." But actually she had many close female friends, and

Natalie Barney was certainly one of them, as the many letters between them indicate. Berthe recalls,

> Gertrude Stein and Miss Toklas were not only invited for the receptions, but for the lunches. We always invited Gertrude Stein for lunches because she was an astonishing personage —physically and every way. At first I was frightened of her ... I took her for a man. When I learned she was a woman, I said: "That's not true." But really they were very intimate friends, very, very intimate.[20]

Natalie pursued friends as ardently as she pursued lovers, and was known to be as constant in friendship as she was inconstant in love. Her relationship with Gertrude was one that she cultivated, slowly and persistently. It came to fruition only in the mid-1920s after they had known of each other for 23 years. Years after the initial invitation to Gertrude to read at her salon—for which Natalie had translated into French some of the pages from Gertrude's *The Making of Americans*—Natalie was still intent on building Franco-American relations between literary women. On 9 January 1931, when Natalie was expecting Gertrude and Alice for tea, she invited along Colette and Lucy Mardrus "and a few others I know are sympathetic to you."

Natalie herself was not completely sympathetic to Gertrude's writing, which had little in common with her own. She wrote, "Being a writer of pensées, I like to find a thought as in a nut- or seashell, but while I make for a point Gertrude seems to proceed by avoiding it ... I cannot see where so simple a dissociation of words from their subject leads us."[21]

Although in no way literary peers—it is probable that Gertrude found Natalie "simple-minded" when it came to literature—the two women would gossip and talk for hours about gastronomy while indulging in cakes at Rumplemeyer's on the rue de Rivoli. They regularly went for neighborhood walks together, accompanied by Gertrude's white poodle, Basket. After Gertrude's death, Natalie recalled these walks in a foreword she wrote for the publication of Gertrude's *As Fine as Melanctha*:

> Often in the evening we would walk together; I, greeted at the door ... by Gertrude's staunch presence, pleasant touch of

hand, well-rounded voice always ready to chuckle. Our talks and walks led us far from war paths. For generally having no axe to grind nor anyone to execute with it, we felt detached and free to wander in our quiet old quarter where, while exercising her poodle, "Basket," we naturally fell into thought and step. Basket, unleashed, ran ahead, a white blur, the ghost of a dog in the moonlit streets:

> Where ghosts and shadows mingle —
> As lovers, lost when single.

The night's enchantment made our conversation as light, iridescent and bouncing as soap bubbles, but as easily exploded when touched upon—so I'll touch on none of them for you, that a bubble may remain a bubble! And perhaps we never said "*d'impérissables choses.*"[22]

Natalie introduced Lily de Clermont-Tonnerre to Gertrude, and the two women became great friends. According to Gertrude Stein's *Autobiography of Alice B. Toklas,*

She and Gertrude Stein pleased one another. They were entirely different in life education and interests but they delighted in each other's understanding.... One day [Lily announced,] the time has now come when you must be made known to a larger public. I myself believe in a larger public. Gertrude Stein too believes in a larger public but the way has always been barred. No, said Madame de Clermont-Tonnerre, the way can be opened. Let us think.

She said it must come from the translation of a big book, an important book. Gertrude Stein suggested the Making of Americans ... That will do exactly, she said. And went away. Finally and not after much delay, Monsieur Bouteleau of Stock saw Gertrude Stein and he decided to publish the book.

Gertrude Stein was not so successful when she similarly solicited a publisher on behalf of Natalie Barney. In 1935, a year after Gertrude's first great "literary success," she used her new, formidable reputation to recommend that Harcourt Brace and Co. publish Natalie's *Aventures de l'esprit.* (Djuna Barnes had tried to find Natalie a publisher in New York in 1930, also without success.) Harcourt Brace wrote back on June 3, 1935 that "it would suffer from comparison with *The Autobiography of Alice B. Toklas* which covers a number of the same people and to a considerable extent the same period, and yet Miss Barney's book is really far less clever and interesting."

When she received the rejection letter from Harcourt, Natalie wrote Gertrude that

> I am lazy enough to be relieved at not having to go over those old "Aventures de l'esprit"—though it would have done Dolly [Wilde] good to go on translating them. I've other fish to fry —small fish that may please the American taste better? I remain very grateful to you for opening Harcourts eyes to my existence. Lots of love N.

The story of Natalie and Gertrude's short-lived falling-out has been told many times. Alice's quip as to where Natalie found her many women—in the lavatory of the Louvre department store—was countered by Natalie's retaliation: she announced that the relationship between Gertrude and Alice was "entirely innocent." But when asked if there was any rivalry between Natalie and Gertrude, the composer Virgil Thomson, who knew both women well, denied it:

> I can't conceive that there was any because they weren't doing the same thing [with their respective salons] ... She'd come to Gertrude's house, and Gertrude would come to hers, and they'd write little *pneumatiques* all the time. Besides which, they were exchanging literary people. If the Sitwells came over and were around Gertrude's, she'd probably take them to Natalie's or have Natalie in or furnish them to Natalie for some soiree. If you've got Edith Sitwell on your hands, you don't want to see her every day.[23]

Edith Sitwell could be tedious. She wrote in 1927 to Gertrude that "We arrive in Paris a week today. Please may a horde of us invade you on Friday afternoon (the 27th) at about 3:30 ..." Natalie and Gertrude found themselves commiserating one evening in Shakespeare and Company, when Edith Sitwell neglected to mention Gertrude's name even once, in a lecture purportedly about Gertrude's writings.

But Edith Sitwell could be helpful as well. She wrote a long article on Gertrude's work for *Vogue* in 1925, "The Works of Gertrude Stein: A Modern Writer Who Brings Literature Nearer to the Apparently Irrational World of Music," and a favorable review of *The Making of Americans* for T.S. Eliot's *The New Criterion.* In 1925 she tried to place Gertrude's *Portraits and Prayers* with several publishers in London, but after meeting with no success, she offered instead to "kill somebody soon,—a reviewer, or possibly a publisher … I should like to do something drastic to the idiot who sent your book back."

According to Natalie's neighbor, Elizabeth Eyre de Lanux, who attended the salon religiously throughout the 1920s and '30s, Gertrude Stein was a regular: "Gertrude Stein was always there—the permanent occupant of right wall center, knees wide-spread, dressed in stout tweeds and mountain climbing boots; she seemed a game warden scrutinizing the birds."[24]

Gertrude's poodle Basket would also attend Natalie's Friday salons, "so perfectly groomed that he seemed to be enameled" according to another salon guest.[25]

A "Rendezvous Among Ladies"

Janet Flanner was also "one of the pillars" of Natalie's salon, as she called it—she was also regularly in attendance at Gertrude's—but denied knowing Natalie very well "because if you weren't in love with her—which I certainly was not, since I brought up the topic—you didn't know as much about her … I never felt that I knew her at all well, really."[26] Perhaps not, but Janet was close to many of the same women in Natalie's circle, including Natalie's lover, Dolly Wilde. Publicly Janet wrote with typical humor and detachment in her *New Yorker* "Letter from Paris" about Oscar Wilde's niece, who showed up at a Parisian party "looking both important and earnest." Privately, however, Dolly sent Janet the following undated letter, which suggests a certain intimacy between the two:

> Dear grey & white Janet Your hair is your fortune and there is a nuance about you that makes you rare and exceptional. Be

RIGHT: Dolly Wilde, whom Janet Flanner found to be more a literary character than a writer of literature.

ABOVE: Journalist Janet Flanner relied on Natalie's personal connections for her *New Yorker* column.

content and comforted. I want to thank you for the bouquet. The pleasure is undescribable—like all enchantment and there is something sad about being unable to tell the secret of pleasure. Be clever enough to enter the core of secret magic and leave me the tedium of explanation … If this letter is incoherent—it is nervousness and hopeless darling.[27]

As a journalist covering life in Paris, Janet relied on Natalie's intimate friendships and far-reaching connections in French society for the inside story which occasionally worked its way into her fortnightly "Letter from Paris" in the *New Yorker*. Natalie supplied the crucial information to Janet of what Mata Hari wore the day she faced the firing squad: contrary to the legend that she wore a mink coat with nothing underneath, she actually "died wearing a neat Amazonian tailored suit, specially made for the occasion, and a pair of new white gloves."

How did Natalie know? Mata Hari was a salon regular. One time she wanted to ride in to the salon on an elephant, but Natalie said, "No, there are cookies and tea, and we can't have an elephant in my garden." So she rode in, nearly naked, on a circus horse instead.

A professional commentator on virtually everything and everyone, Janet Flanner was reticent on the subject of Natalie Barney, claiming that she didn't know much, that she was "a very spotty recollector," and that Natalie "is a perfect example of an enchanting person not to write about." Yet as an old woman she did recall with charming detail both Natalie and her damp, *démodé* house, from the paintings of nymphs hanging from the ceiling, to the luxurious pale blue silk sheets Natalie used. Janet Flanner's recollections of the salon focus on the social and sexual rather than literary aspects of the proceedings:

> … Introductions, conversation, tea, excellent cucumber sandwiches [in tribute to those served in Oscar Wilde's *The Importance of Being Earnest*], divine little cakes Berthe baked, and then the result: a new rendezvous among ladies who had taken a fancy to each other or wished to see each other again.[28]

Because of Natalie's overt lesbianism, many women, from Janet Flanner to Djuna Barnes to Gisèle Freund, later played down their association with her, although letters and other evidence survive to contradict their denials of friendship. Gisèle Freund claims she was warned by

ABOVE: "Una, Lady Troubridge" by Romaine Brooks, 1924. Romaine found
the male posturing of Radclyffe Hall and Una Troubridge ridiculous, and painted
Una as a virtual caricature — after which the friendship was permanently strained.

Adrienne Monnier not to attend Natalie's salon, even though Adrienne and Sylvia were often in attendance themselves:

> [Natalie] received every Friday her friends. It was not considered decent to go there. And so Adrienne said, "You better not go there." She never said why, but … I didn't go. I never met these people.[29]

The reason may well have been to protect Gisèle, not from indecency but from Natalie herself. Sylvia and Adrienne privately thought of Natalie as "the breaker of so many hearts—a real killer, Miss B."[30]

The Well of Loneliness

Sylvia Beach makes a point of establishing in her memoirs that she was *not* at Natalie Barney's salon on one particularly risqué evening:

> At Miss Barney's one met the ladies with high collars and monocles, though Miss Barney herself was so feminine. Unfortunately, I missed the chance to make the acquaintance at her salon of the authoress of *The Well of Loneliness*, in which she concluded that if inverted couples could be united at the altar, all their problems would be solved.[31]

It is likely that Gertrude and Alice *were* at Natalie's on this occasion, for, improbable though it may seem, they became friendly with Radclyffe Hall and Una Troubridge around this time, or at least friendly enough to receive postcards from the two English women who were staying at the Grand Hotel Bristol in Merano, Italy shortly after passing through Paris.

Although Radclyffe Hall ("John") and her lover Una, Lady Troubridge seem to have been close friends with Natalie and Romaine for a time, they were more frequently spotted, with their monocles and long cigarette holders, at the Café des Deux Magots than at Natalie's salon.

Radclyffe Hall reputedly hated the idea of promiscuity, for which Natalie was famous. Indeed, she portrayed Natalie as Valerie in her famous, controversial lesbian novel, *The Well of Loneliness*, first published in 1928:

Most of her sketches were written in French, for among other things Valerie was bilingual; she was also quite rich, an American uncle had had the foresight to leave her his fortune; she was also quite young, being just over thirty, and … good-looking. She lived her life in great calmness of spirit, for nothing worried and few things distressed her. She was firmly convinced that in this ugly age one should strive to the top of one's bent after beauty … she was *libre penseuse* when it came to the heart; her love affairs would fill quite three volumes, even after they had been expurgated. Great men had loved her, great writers had written about her, one had died, it was said, because she refused him, but Valerie was not attracted to men …

The Well of Loneliness goes on to describe the first impressions of a literary salon, clearly modeled on Natalie's:

So pleasant was it to be made to feel welcome by all these clever and interesting people—and clever they were there was no denying; in Valerie's salon the percentage of brains was generally well above average. For together with those who themselves being normal, had long put intellects above bodies, were writers, painters, musicians and scholars, men and women who, set apart from their birth, had determined to hack out a niche in existence.

Romaine figured in an earlier novel of Radclyffe Hall's, *The Forge,* and as a minor character in *The Well of Loneliness;* she also appeared in a book by Bryher. Yet her largest and most unflattering literary role was in another novel published in 1928, Compton MacKenzie's *Extraordinary Women.* Focusing on a group of lesbians in Capri, *Extraordinary Women* is as explicit a novel as *The Well of Loneliness.* Unlike *The Well,* however, which was burned in the cellars of Scotland Yard, *Extraordinary Women* met with no trouble at all from the censors, no doubt because it ridiculed lesbianism more than it promoted tolerance or understanding—which presumably is what a good novel about lesbians should do.

The censors did not seem to care that the lesbian love in *The Well of Loneliness* was portrayed negatively, as distressing or even harrowing—but Radclyffe Hall's friends and contemporaries certainly did.

Colette wrote to Una Troubridge (who had adapted Colette's *Chéri* for the stage) that the characters' emotions in *The Well of Loneliness* were wrong: "an abnormal man or woman should never feel abnormal, quite the contrary."[32] Janet Flanner thought the book's premise was misguided: "her whole analysis was false and based upon the fact that the heroine's mother, when expecting her, had hoped for a boy baby, which as a daughter, Miss Hall interpreted literally."[33]

Janet, at the time, held her usually scathing tongue when it came to reviewing the book in print. She avoided any mention of its literary merits, and joked instead about its value as contraband: "Its biggest daily sale [in Paris] takes place from the news vendor's cart serving the de luxe trains for London, La Flèche d'or, at the Gare du Nord." When a theatrical version of the novel was staged in Paris, the kindest thing Janet could find to write in her review is that the character of Stephen Gordon "made up in costume what she lacked in psychology."

Romaine did not object to her appearance in Bryher's novel, and wrote, "What a pleasure again to see fragment in your book! Was a bit shy at first—so much about myself, but now am so glad. When will you be in Paris?" Yet she was less than pleased with *The Well of Loneliness,* and not only because of her own depiction. To Natalie she revealed her honest response: "a ridiculous book, trite, superficial, as was to be expected. A digger-up of worms with the pretension of a distinguished archaeologist ... She has watched me with the eye of a sparrow who sees no further than the window-pane." No further than the window-pane—the ultimate insult from an artist whose gaze seemed to bore right through the body and into one's soul, so much so that Romaine has been dubbed "The Thief of Souls."

The Portrait Not Painted

Throughout the 1920s and '30s, Romaine had designs on Gertrude's soul. She begged Gertrude to sit for her portrait, pleading that

> Since my last portrait painted several years ago no one has
> occupied so important a place in my mind as yourself. I have
> always wanted to paint you as you know; but tendencies
> some-how stronger than all else forced me to work at quite

LEFT: Not one to allow the sweep of fascism across Europe to interfere with her personal pleasures, Natalie kept up her membership in the Paris racing club in 1939.

other things: subconscious drawings and even "memoires" for which I have no particular talent. Now your portrait comes again forcibly to the foreground …

There was always one excuse or another, and in the end it never came about. Once when the two couples were spending an afternoon together in Bilignin at Gertrude's and Alice's country house, Romaine was suddenly inspired to paint the whole group, but Natalie had other plans:

> Another meeting with this inseparable couple took place in their *jardin de cure* at Bilignin, on another summer afternoon … The four of us—for Romaine Brooks had come along with me—and Basket, all curves and capers, lent a circus effect to the scene …
>
> Meanwhile Romaine, contemplating our group and finding it "paintable," wished to start a picture of it then and there, before the light or her inspiration should fade. But I the disturbing element of the party, because of a clock in my mind and in duty bound to pleasures, insisted that Romaine and I were due elsewhere. So this picture of us all was left unpainted: *mea culpa!*[34]

During the Second World War, Romaine again wrote to Gertrude: "Often think of portrait not yet painted. Is your new poodle like Basket?"

Shortly after Gertrude's death in 1946, as Natalie was trying to place a painting of Romaine's in the Tate Gallery in London, she suddenly recalled Romaine's desire to paint Gertrude's portrait. To Alice she wrote, "What a pity that [Romaine] never did Gertrude's portrait, but then the Picasso is and should perhaps remain unique." Gertrude probably preferred it this way anyway, as she felt Picasso's portrait "is the only reproduction of me which is always I."[35]

Natalie's friendship with Gertrude and Alice during the war years indicates a deep gulf between her genuine sympathy and concern for those she knew personally and her complete insensitivity, prejudice, and brutishness when it came to the rest of humanity. Her acceptance of the popular trend of anti-Semitism was not mitigated by her close friendship with two American Jews in hiding in the French countryside. Under the influence of her fascist and equally politically confused friend, Ezra Pound, who was living in Mussolini's Italy, Natalie decided the Axis had "superior leadership and cause" and in 1939 she moved with Romaine to Italy, "that Latin sister, until ours comes to her senses, finds herself again and puts her house in order."

There is no question that Natalie's political views were indefensible. She was always muddled and misguided when it came to politics, but clear as a bell when it came to friendships and personal loyalties. Her anti-Semitic views were abstractions, incongruous with her feelings about people she knew (including her beloved mother, who was half-Jewish). From Italy she sent poems and letters to Gertrude and Alice, signing them "with love to you both, from both [her and Romaine], your not unhappy exile (as the verses enclosed prove!)."

Many decades later, when Alice died, she was buried in the same grave Gertrude occupied in Père Lachaise cemetery in Paris. Romaine and Natalie found this so romantic that they devised a similar joint-burial plan—but it never came to pass since Natalie, whose art was love, had one more masterpiece in mind. She fell in love with Janice Lahovary, wife of a diplomat, who left her husband and two sons in order to care for Natalie in her old age. The novelist and journalist Germaine Beaumont found it "marvelous, not to find love at 88, but to find a co-respondent."[36] Romaine, who had put up with Natalie's infidelity for over fifty years, was less enthusiastic. Initially she tolerated the arrangement, and even visited Natalie at Janice Lahovary's home (where a lift was installed for Natalie who could no long climb stairs). But one day she finally had had enough.

Romaine told Berthe, who was still Natalie's housekeeper and confidante: "It was all over from the minute that creature managed to slip between us. I thought I was going to end my days with Miss Barney. Now it's impossible. Let her leave me in peace!" Both women were in their nineties when Romaine broke off the relationship, refused Natalie's desperate apologies and love letters, and died alone in the south of France.

Natalie's tireless heart, which had long ruled her body, mind, and soul, was finally broken. She might otherwise have lived forever, but died soon after her beloved Romaine.

ABOVE: Natalie Barney in middle age, still the Amazon.

4

CITY OF DARK NIGHTS

Perhaps the greatest enigma of Paris literary life between the wars was, and remains, Djuna Barnes. Men and women of all persuasions found her irresistible, falling for her considerable beauty, glamour, intelligence, and sharp wit. Today, darker and more disturbing qualities than these continue to attract readers and scholars to her life and work. But, then as now, it is virtually impossible to extricate a "real" identity from the myth that has become Djuna Barnes — partly because she herself believed in the myth and left little behind to contradict it, and partly because her life offers up the kind of Hollywood or tabloid legend our culture loves so well. Like Tennessee Williams, Rainer Werner Fassbinder, or Jane Bowles, Djuna Barnes brings together the familiar but endlessly fascinating scenarios of tortured creativity, tragic homosexuality, and the genius drowning in booze. While her life alternately substantiates and invalidates these scenarios, the "facts" of her life surpass anything that Hollywood could have dreamt up.

Born in New York State in 1892, Djuna Barnes grew up in a "bohemian" household which included not only her grandmother, parents, and their three children, but one of her father's several mistresses and *her* various children. This family has been called sexually unconventional but is perhaps more aptly described as exploitative and

LEFT: Djuna Barnes "A beautiful woman, very tall, very 'majestic' she was a real character. Really." —Berthe Cleyrergue, housekeeper to Natalie Barney.

DJUNA LITTLE   DJUNA BIG

ABOVE: Haunted by the traumas of her childhood, Djuna drew this double portrait of herself as simultaneously woman and child.

sexually abusive. Her closest "parent" was her grandmother, Zadel Barnes Budington, herself an early feminist and prolific writer, yet it is likely that this closeness bordered on incest—certainly the many letters Zadel wrote to Djuna are pornographic, and make reference to sexual activity between them. Her father attempted to rape the teenaged Djuna, an event she recounted years later to her friend Emily Coleman. When she reached seventeen, her father, with her mother's collusion, gave her as a sexual sacrifice to the brother of his live-in mistress (who later became his second wife)—a parental betrayal that has been variously described as a marriage to, or a rape by, her much older uncle, although no legal documents verifying a marriage have been found. Not surprisingly, the traumas of her childhood haunted her for the rest of her life, resurfacing, through various literary forms and strategies, in her early drama *The Dove* as well as in her major works: *Ryder* (1928), *Nightwood* (1936), and *The Antiphon* (1958).

In 1910, at the age of 18, Djuna started publishing poetry. Two years later she moved to Greenwich Village, began art studies at the Pratt Institute, and found a reporting job with the *Brooklyn Eagle,* thus embarking on a journalistic career that would continue intermittently for 25 years.

Although Djuna did not consider her journalism as serious writing and wrote out of financial necessity, even in this she engaged in the extraordinary and the spectacular. She crawled around a female gorilla's cage in an attempt to commune with her; she underwent forced

RIGHT: Djuna Barnes pioneered a kind of participatory journalism: here she is being rescued by a fireman's rope from atop a skyscraper.

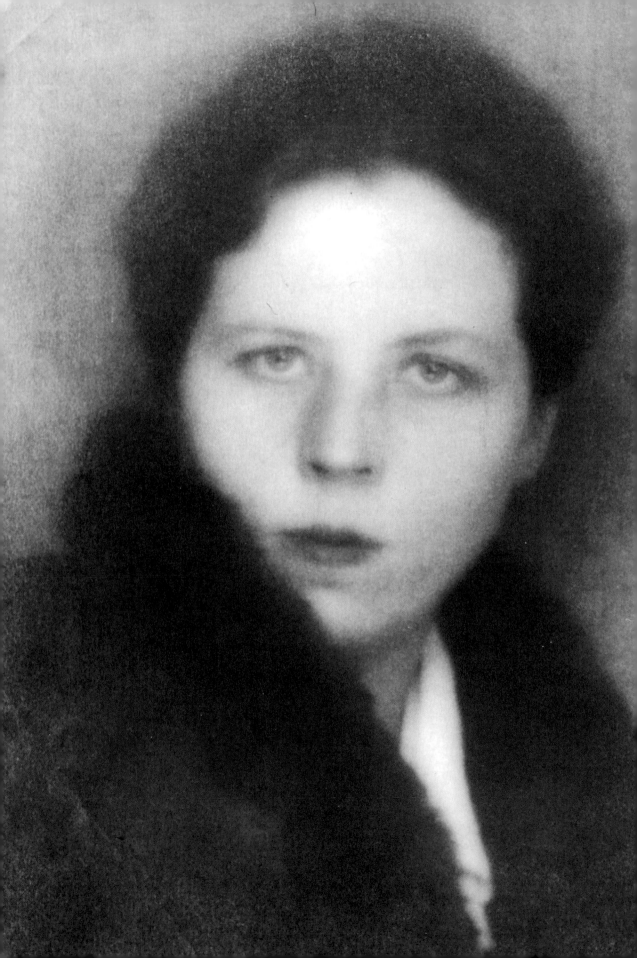

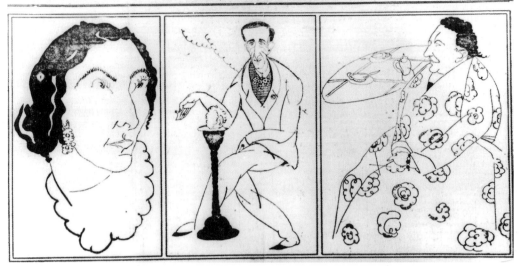

ABOVE: Djuna drew these caricatures of three personalities in Paris: the poet Mina Loy who became her close friend, the homosexual artist Marsden Hartley with whom it is rumored she had a brief affair, and "spiritual mother of all the Modernists" as she was called here, Gertrude Stein. Djuna never forgave Gertrude for admiring her legs—a sure indication to Djuna that Gertrude did not also admire her writing.

feeding for a sympathetic article on English suffragettes. Under the pseudonym Lydia Steptoe, she wrote several feminist satires on women's conventional roles. But always she distinguished these pieces from her private, creative, and noncommercial writing: poetry (most of which from this period has been lost), short stories, and one-act plays, which were produced by the avant-garde Provincetown Players in Greenwich Village.

The details of her life between the years 1912 and 1920 are scant and conflicting—something she would have enjoyed. Obsessed with privacy, she concealed and contradicted biographical facts, even while the deeper truths of her life invariably surfaced through her writing. We do know that in these years she was in love with women and men, apparently having had a brief marriage to writer Courtenay Lemon after the "arranged" marriage to her uncle ended, although no legal record for this second marriage exists either. Her lovers from this time included, possibly, the homosexual painter Marsden Hartley

LEFT: Djuna Barnes: "Certainly she was one of the most talented and, I think, one of the most fascinating literary figures in the Paris of the twenties."—Sylvia Beach

(although *his* biographer disputes it), the poet Mary Pyre (Djuna nursed Mary until she died in 1919 of tuberculosis), and, briefly, Jane Heap, coeditor with Margaret Anderson of *The Little Review*. *The Little Review* had moved from Chicago to New York and then on to Paris, and had published Djuna widely in these years. It is rumored that Djuna hated Margaret Anderson for taking Jane Heap away from her; Djuna's dislike did not wane when the three all found themselves settled in Paris.

It was her writings in *The Little Review* as well as a chapbook of eight poems and five drawings, *The Book of Repulsive Women* (a satire on the way men look at women's bodies), which brought Djuna's reputation, as both writer and visual artist, to Paris before her actual arrival in 1919. She settled into the Hotel Angleterre on the rue Jacob, adorned in Peggy Guggenheim's elegant black cape and other cast-off clothing, and each morning she wrote in bed.

Djuna had a brief affair with Natalie Barney, a rite of passage not uncommon among attractive female arrivals in Paris at that time. Djuna became a regular "fixture" at Natalie's lesbian soirées and drew on this circle of women to write *Ladies Almanack*. Although Djuna's sexual practice was not fixed, her writing was: from the outset, it utilized lesbian-coded language and lesbian themes, culminating in the particularly explicit *Ladies Almanack,* privately printed in Paris in 1928, and published under the pseudonym, "A Lady of Fashion." Natalie Barney had written in January of that year to Richard Aldington, ex-husband of the poet H.D., about publishing it, arguing on the basis of potential sales:

> All ladies fit to figure in such an almanack should of course be eager to have a copy, and all gentlemen disapproving of them. Then the public might, with a little judicious treatment, include those lingering on the border of such islands and those eager to be ferried across.[1]

But, in the end, it was printed by Contact Editions, Robert McAlmon's press (Djuna felt its name to be a misnomer as it didn't have much contact to or with anything). Robert McAlmon had been married to

LEFT: "Djuna was a very haughty lady, quick on uptake, and with a wise-cracking tongue that I was far too discreet to try and rival . . ." — Robert McAlmon

ABOVE: Three of Djuna Barnes's drawings for *Ladies Almanack.*

Bryher for a time, a financial arrangement designed to free Bryher from the clutches of her enormously wealthy family. The divorce settlement of £14,000 which he received from her shipping magnate father earned him the nickname Robert McAlimony and enabled him to establish Contact Editions. So it is ironic that *Ladies Almanack*, a far more radical lesbian book than Radclyffe Hall's *The Well of Loneliness*, published in the same year, was unwittingly financed by Bryher's family.

Djuna Barnes dismissed *Ladies Almanack* as a "slight satiric wigging" and "jollity," and claimed it was written "in an idle hour" for a "very special audience." The most immediate special audience for it was her lover Thelma Wood, an American silverpoint artist and sculptor whom Djuna had met in 1920 or 1921; Djuna apparently wrote it to amuse Thelma during a stay in hospital. But Djuna's efforts on behalf of the book belie her attempts, later in her life, to trivialize it. She not only hand-colored 50 of the 1050 copies, but hawked it herself on the streets of Paris when its distributor fell through. Sylvia Beach also helped by carrying it in Shakespeare and Company.

Despite the lack of distributor, *Ladies Almanack* quickly became the talk of the town, with much speculation as to who was who.

While the book is riddled with private references, innuendoes, and allusions that make for amusing, if baffling, reading, we are fortunate in that Natalie Barney and Janet Flanner both annotated their copies.

NATALIE BARNEY: DAME EVANGELINE MUSSET

born lesbian and on a mission to recruit others, who says to her father

Am I not took after your very Desire, and is it not the more commendable, seeing that I do it without the Tools for the Trade, and yet nothing complain?

MINA LOY: PATIENCE SCALPEL

the one staunch heterosexual, she

belongs to this Almanack for one Reason only, that from Beginning to End, Top to Bottom, inside and out, she could not understand Women and their Ways as they were about her, above her and before her.

(Nonetheless, by August even Patience Scalpel starts to make a move towards women.)

DOLLY WILDE: DOLL FURIOUS

… Amid the rugs Dame Musset brought Doll Furious to a certainty.
"… Ah!" [Dame Musset] sighed, "there were many such when I was a
Girl, and in particular I recall one dear old Countess who was not to be
convinced until I, fervid with Truth, had finally so floored her in every
capacious Room of that dear ancestral Home, that I knew to a Button,
how every Ticking was made! And what a lack of Art there is in the
Upholstery Trade, for that they do not finish off the under Parts of Sofas
and Chairs … There should … be Trade for Contacts, guarding that on
which the Lesbian Eye must, in its March through Life, rest itself."

ROMAINE BROOKS: CYNIC SAL

"The Night-Light of Love," said Saint Musset, "burns I think me in the
slightly muted Crevices of all Women … There is one … on whom I have
had a Weather Eye these many years.… Her Name is writ from here to
Sicily, as Cynic Sal. She dressed like a Coachman … but she drives an
empty Hack. And that is one Woman," she said, "who shall yet find me as
Fare, and if at the Journey's end, she still cracks as sharp a Whip, and has
never once descended the Driver's Seat to put her Head within to see what
rumpled meaning there sits, why she may sing for her Pains, I shall get off
at London and find me another who has somewhat of a budding Care for
a Passenger."

TWO BRITISH WOMEN, RADCLYFFE HALL: TILLY TWEED-IN-BLOOD

sported a Stetson and believed in Marriage (between women; she wanted
to put the question to the House of Lords), and

UNA TROUBRIDGE: LADY BUCK-AND-BALK

sported a Monocle and believed in Spirits:

They came to the Temple of the Good Dame Musset, and they sat to Tea,
and this is what they said: "Just because woman falls, in this Age, to
Woman, does that mean that we are not to recognize Morals? What has
England done to legalize these Passions? Nothing! Should she not be
brought to Task, that never once through her gloomy Weather have two
dear Doves been seen approaching their bridal Laces, to pace, in stately
Splendor up the Altar Aisle, there to be United in Similarity, under mutual
Vows of Loving, Honoring, and Obeying, while the One and the Other

fumble in that nice Temerity, for the
equal gold Bands that shall make of one
a Wife, and the other a Bride?"

JANET FLANNER AND SOLITA SOLANO: THE MESSENGERS NIP & TUCK

They alert Dame Musset to women she
might recruit.

"We come … to let you know there is a
Flall loose in the Town who is crying
from Corner to Niche, in that lament-
ing Herculean Voice that sounds to us
like a Sister lost, for certainly it is not
the Whine of Motherhood, but a more
mystic, sodden Sighing. So it seems to
us, as Members of the Sect, we should
deliver to you this piece of Information, that you may repair what has
never been damaged."

ABOVE: Thelma Wood, "Berlin 1921," which
is where and when she first met Djuna.

"It shall be done, and done most wily well," said the Dame … "Where
was she last seen, and which way going? … To scent, we will chase her into
a very Tangle of Temptation!"

DUCHESSE DE CLERMONT-TONNERRE: DUCHESS CLITORESSA OF NATESCOURT

Already, when Evangeline appeared to Tea to the Duchess Clitoressa of
Natescourt, women on the way … would snatch their Skirts from Con-
tamination …

Ladies Almanack has been called a lesbian creation myth, beginning with the birth
of "the first Woman born with a Difference." Ridiculing the sexology of its day,
it turns Havelock Ellis's image of the dangerous lesbian seducer into, as claimed
in the foreword to the most recent edition, "'one Grand Red Cross' for wom-
en's sexual relief!" *Ladies Almanack* also eschews the "lesbianism as cruel trick of
nature" stance of *The Well of Loneliness,* offering it instead as a welcome departure from heterosexual aggression. Rather than pleading for sympathy or tolerance, *Ladies Almanack* relies on lesbian innuendo and codes to speak to lesbians

INVITATION

TELMA WOOD

DESSINS

DU 29 OCTOBRE AU 10 NOVEMBRE

AUX

QUATRE CHEMINS

18, RUE GODOT-DE-MAUROY, 18
PARIS (IX·)   (MADELEINE)

VERNISSAGE
Le Vendredi 29 Octobre, à 15 heures

LEFT: This exhibition of Thelma's drawings in 1926 "caused much excitement" according to the *New York Telegram,* which found her work to "have a delicate exotic beauty all their own."

directly, leaving others to make of it what they will. "Showing their Signs and their tides; their Moons and their Changes; the Seasons as well as a full Record of diurnal and nocturnal Distempers," *Ladies Almanack* celebrates the lesbian body.

There is nothing in *Ladies Almanack* and, indeed, little in the bits and pieces we know of her life during the early and mid-1920s to fit the images of tragic homosexual or tortured writer we've come to associate with Djuna Barnes. The first few years with Thelma Wood were genuinely joyful ones. From 1922, the two women lived together on the Left Bank, first at 173 Boulevard St. Germain and later at 9 rue St. Romain. Djuna's letters to Natalie Barney describe their life together as peaceful and productive: "We are very quiet: Thelma is painting, I trying a novel, a short story, and a play, all at once!" The following year, Bryher visited them and reported to H.D. that the two women were happy together. They conceived of their relationship as an idyllic family, with Djuna as "Momma" or "Junie" and Thelma as "Papa" or "Simon"; their cat Dilly was a surrogate child. They wrote each other loving letters:

> "I love you my very own—
> forever —
>   Simon
>
> I also kiss you a great many kisses."

And Djuna's most autobiographical novel, *Ryder* (1928), which chronicles her unusual family history, was dedicated to T.W.

Before the city of light became a city of dark nights for Djuna Barnes, she was an integral part of the vibrant female artistic community that congregated not only at Natalie Barney's Friday salon but also informally at each other's homes. Janet Flanner regularly retreated to the home of Noel Murphy in the village of Orgeval in order to escape the pressures of Paris, and was highly selective about whom she and Noel would invite there, but Djuna was among the inner circle. A frequent guest, she could often be found in their garden, sunbathing in the nude. Writer Kathryn Hulme described first seeing Djuna with Janet Flanner and Solita Solano at the Café Flore, where the three women, drinking martinis in tailored suits and white gloves, looked like three Fates.[2]

One of Djuna's closest friends was Mina Loy. Born in London, Mina was a woman graced with, or perhaps burdened by, multiple talents: she was by turns a poet, painter, playwright, actress, and designer. To the extent that she was known in her day, it was mostly as a Modernist poet, but it was Modernism with a twist. Her poems, published in *The Little Review,* combined her literary experimentation with an interest in feminist themes, while her novels also explored aspects of her Jewish identity. Ezra Pound, the self-appointed authority on Modernist poetry, announced that he had read quite a bit of "rubbish" by her but called one of her works "the utterance of clever people in despair, or hovering upon the brink of that precipice …"—faint praise. Perhaps because she actually lived on that brink, Mina Loy saw only two volumes published during her lifetime: *Lunar Baedecker,* which, like Djuna's *Ladies Almanack,* was published by Robert McAlmon's Contact Editions (1923), and, much later, *Lunar Baedecker and Time-tables* (1958).

Eugene Jolas, editor of *transition,* wrote about Mina Loy's work, admiring the fact that it took years for her to produce anything: "In this age of mechanical over-production and standardized esthetics, it is a real delight to meet a writer who works with almost Stoic slowness … 'One must have lived ten years to write a poem,' she said."[3]

It is ironic that Mina Loy would so admire the prolific Gertrude Stein, who wrote daily at breakneck speed, virtually without revision (although according to Virgil Thomson she first "waited always for

the moment when she would be full of readiness to write").[4] Privately Mina Loy wrote Gertrude intimate letters: "Dearest and only Gertrude … I long to see you. Most love to you both." Publicly she honored her in a poem published in *Transatlantic Review:*

Curie
of the laboratory
of vocabulary
she crushed
the tonnage
of consciousness
congealed to phrases
to extract
a radium of the word.

Mina Loy was a regular at both Natalie Barney's and Gertrude Stein's salons, where she was occasionally accompanied by Djuna Barnes. In 1927, she gave a talk at Natalie's about Gertrude Stein and on a different afternoon read from her own work, thus earning herself a place in Djuna Barnes's *Ladies Almanack* as the sole heterosexual woman, Patience Scalpel.

Mina had married a fellow art student in 1904, but they became estranged, both took other lovers, and eventually divorced, leaving her with two children (a third had died in infancy). Moving between Paris, Florence, and New York, she met the poet/boxer/draft dodger Arthur Cravan in 1917, who became the great love of her life. Arthur Cravan was a hero to the Surrealists and Dadaists in Paris; this gave Mina Loy a certain, dubious stature among them when she returned to Paris in the twenties. Her romance with the wild Arthur resulted in another child and enormous heartache. When she married him in Mexico City in 1918, it marked the end, rather than the beginning, of their relationship. He disappeared shortly after in the desert; his body was never found.

When *The Little Review* sent out a questionnaire to all previous contributors for their last issue, Mina answered the question "What was the happiest moment in your life?" by saying, "Every moment I

LEFT: Thelma in the early idyllic days of her relationship with Djuna.

ABOVE: The close friendship between Djuna Barnes and Mina Loy was rooted in their shared artistic and emotional temperaments.

spent with Arthur Cravan." For the next question, "and the unhappiest?" she wrote "the rest of the time"—for her that would be another forty years.

Unlike the other Modernist women on the Left Bank, Mina Loy ended up back in Paris as a single mother, now with two children to support (her first husband had taken one of the three). This she did by opening a lampshade design business with the financial backing of Peggy Guggenheim. She had ingenious designs for inventions as well, including children's games, window washers, and other practical items, none of which she ever patented. In her Modernist literary efforts, her stunning beauty, her numerous gifts as a visual artist, and her prolonged agony in matters of the heart, one can readily see the basis of Mina Loy's close friendship with Djuna Barnes.

Although her closest friends were women, Djuna Barnes was also admired by many of the male writers and artists who congregated in Paris in the twenties. She was respected as a writer rather than because she was in a position to publish, introduce, distribute, publicize, or otherwise assist the men. This respect for her writing didn't necessarily correspond with comprehension, but then clarity was not high on the list of Modernist literary requirements, as Janet Flanner tells us:

> Djuna had written a play that she showed to T.S. Eliot; he told her that it contained the most splendid archaic language he had ever had the pleasure of reading but that, frankly, he couldn't make head or tail of its drama. She gave it to me to read, and I told her, with equal candor, that it was the most sonorous vocabulary I had ever read but that I did not understand jot or title of

RIGHT: Mina Loy's design for one of her many lamps. She had a good eye for design but a bad head for business.

125

what it was saying. With withering scorn, she said, "I never expected to find that you were as stupid as Tom Eliot." I thanked her for the only compliment she had ever given me.[5]

The intrepid Djuna Barnes not only was on a first-name basis with T.S. Eliot but, according to Janet Flanner, was the only person allowed to call James Joyce "Jim"—something even Hemingway didn't dare. The ever proper Mr. Joyce, however, continued to call her Miss Barnes, just as he called Sylvia (as she was known to everyone else), Miss Beach. Joyce, "with the strange formality of a polyglot genius in exile, remained Mr. Joyce" to everyone besides Djuna Barnes.[6]

Soon after her arrival in Paris, Djuna wrote an essay for *Vanity Fair* about her first encounters with James Joyce, whom she clearly admired from the start:

LEFT: Letter to Djuna Barnes from James Joyce

And then, one day, I came to Paris. Sitting in the café of the Deux Magots, which faces the little church of St. Germain des Prés, I saw approaching out of the fog and damp, a tall man, with head slightly lifted and slightly turned, giving to the wind an orderly distemper of red and black hair, which descended sharply into a scant wedge on an out-thrust chin …

It has been my pleasure to talk to him many times during my four months in Paris. We have talked of rivers and of religion, of the instinctive genius of the church which chose, for the singing of its hymns, the voice without "overtones"—the voice of the eunuch. We have talked of women; about women he seems a bit disinterested. Were I vain, I should say he is afraid of them, but I am certain he is only a little skeptical of their existence. We have talked of Ibsen, of Strindberg, Shakespeare … We have talked of death, of rats, of horses, the sea; languages, climates and offerings. Of artists and of Ireland …

He has, if we admit Joyce to be Stephen [Daedelus], done as he said he would do. "I will not serve that which I no longer believe, whether it call itself my home, my fatherland, or my church; and I will try to express myself in my art as freely as I can, using for my defense the only arms I allow myself to use: silence, exile and cunning."

This is somehow Joyce, and one wonders if, at last, Ireland has created her man.

When James Joyce's *Ulysses* was published in 1922, it was considered *the* Modernist masterpiece. Reading it piecemeal in *The Little Review*, Djuna despaired of her future as a writer: "I shall never write another line. Who has the nerve after this?"[7] Critics later berated her for imitating (and poorly at that) Joyce's style, even though Sylvia Beach, who knew Joyce's style better than anyone, claimed emphatically that Djuna's work "did not resemble that of any other writer of the time."[8] Although he must be considered an influence on Djuna's work, her writing influenced his as well, particularly *Finnegans Wake,* published three years after *Nightwood.* Joyce himself didn't feel that Djuna's writing was derivative of his—he gave her one of the early unnumbered press copies of *Ulysses* and considered her among the select few with whom he would discuss his work. Apparently sharing her low opinion of journalism, he wrote to her with the following "literary advice": "A writer must never write about the extraordinary. That is for the journalist."

Djuna Barnes did not take his advice. In her life and her writing, she was consistently drawn to the extraordinary. In the writing of *Nightwood,* her greatest work, she began closest to home, with her relationship with Thelma—which by now was not ordinary by any standards—and over the years kept rewriting and transforming her novel towards the extraordinary, the fantastic, and the bizarre.

Although *Nightwood* is larger, more complex, and finally far more interesting as a novel than the "facts" of Djuna and Thelma, one can readily see its autobiographical origins, especially in its tracing of the painful, destructive path upon which she and Thelma had embarked. The initial relationship between Nora and Robin in *Nightwood* clearly recalls the early, idyllic days between Djuna and Thelma.

> She stayed with Nora until mid-winter. Two spirits were
> working in her, love and anonymity. Yet they were so
> "haunted" of each other that separation was impossible. Nora
> bought an apartment in the rue du Cherche-Midi. Robin had
> chosen it. In the passage of their lives together, every object in
> the garden, every item in the house, every word they spoke,
> attested to their mutual love, the combining of their humors.

By 1924 or early 1925, the romance between Djuna and Thelma began to turn increasingly volatile, strained by their excessive drinking and Thelma's promiscuity. After one particularly heavy night, Thelma proposed marriage to Peggy Guggenheim.

More disturbing to Djuna was Thelma's affair with the poet and playwright Edna St. Vincent Millay, an old acquaintance of Djuna's from the Provincetown Players days, who came temporarily to Paris to escape her supposedly "sexually liberated" lifestyle in Greenwich Village. There was no love lost between Djuna and "Vincent" (as Millay was often called) even before the affair with Thelma Wood. Djuna's biographer, Andrew Field, claims that this was because "Barnes was jealous of the success of Millay."[9] When Edna St. Vincent Millay wrote her most overtly lesbian play, *The Lamp and the Bell,* based on her intense college relationship with Charlotte ("Charlie") Babcock, she wrote to her sister Norma Millay: "But don't let any of the

ABOVE: A sketch of James Joyce by Djuna Barnes, n.d. She inadvertently put his eye patch over the wrong eye.

ABOVE: "Red cheeks. Auburn hair. Grey eyes, ever sparkling with delight and mischief . . . : that's the real Djuna as she walks down Fifth Avenue, or sips her black coffee, a cigarette in hand, in the Café Lafayette." —Guido Bruno

Provincetown Players get hold of it to read. I mean this most seriously. They would hate it, & make fun of it, & and old Djuna Barnes would rag you about it, hoping it would get to me."[10] With her stunning red hair, her lovers of both genders and all persuasions, her writing which she divided into "serious" plays and poetry, or income-generating journalism and feminist satire (also under a pseudonym), and her own "tragic streak" of alcoholism and, later, extreme isolation, Edna St. Vincent Millay's life oddly paralleled Djuna Barnes's.

According to Berthe Cleyrergue:

> Thelma Wood was living with Djuna in Natalie Barney's house when I met her in 1925. It was a complete disaster. For a month, they left everything everywhere. It was the beginning of the end for the two of them, and when Thelma was the first to leave, Djuna went to the Hotel Angleterre, rue Jacob, and that is where she began to drink and drink and drink. They phoned me from the Hotel Angleterre to come and get her. I brought her back to the rue Jacob and there I nursed her for a month . . .[11]

[left margin handwritten facsimile of letter]

In June 1927, the first break in the relationship occurred when Thelma left for America; she wrote this heart-wrenching letter from the ship:

Dearest one—You said something just as I was leaving that makes things seem a little less terrible—maybe you didn't mean it—you said it so softly—that we could meet in New York and maybe Simon would be different. But you see how Silly Simon must clutch on anything to make him stronger—you see I can't think of anything ahead that doesn't mean you —

I keep saying, "Simon you've got to be a man and take your medicine" —but then always in my head goes "there is no Simon and no Junie" and I can't bear it and go crazy … I feel so shy at saying anything for fear it sounds like excusing which God knows I don't—but I've thought over it all and I think if I didn't drink maybe things wouldn't have suffered [?]—as that is usually when I get involved [with someone else]. Now Simon will not touch one drop till you come to America and I'll have my exhibition done—and I'll try and be financially independent—and then maybe if you still care—and look him over—and he again looks sweet to you Perhaps we could try it a new way—and if you will I will never again as long as you love me take one small drop of anything stronger than tea.

Although nothing—not the drinking, the affairs, nor the financial dependency—changed in their relationship, the letter was apparently persuasive, for they were reunited in Paris later that year. They made a home together at 9 rue St. Romain (which Djuna was able to buy from the proceeds of *Ryder)*. But Thelma's penchant for other women drove them to a torturous breakup. This time Thelma wrote Djuna:

Signification des principales indications éventuelles
pouvant figurer en tête de l'adresse.

D ... = Urgent.   XPx ..... = Exprès payé.
AR.. = Remettre contre reçu.   NUIT.... = Remettre même
PC.. = Accusé de Réception.   pendant la nuit.
RP. = Réponse payée.   JOUR.... = Remettre seulement
TC.. = Télégramme collationné.   pendant le jour.
MP. = Remettre en mains propres.   OUVERT = Remettre ouvert.

Via WESTERN UNION

SIMON LOVES YOU DARLING HE WILL GO MAD IF YOU DONT SEND

HIM SOME WORD LOVE

ABOVE: Waiting impatiently for some word from Djuna...

Djuna beautiful—... I knew I had lost you—I realized every misdeed committed in eight years would come back—that every one in Paris would be against me ... The knowing you saw us, I had said such terrible things I hated myself.... I did not want such a thing to be known between us—something I did not care about—It seemed a shame for foolishness to spoil us—I wanted no *acknowledged* disloyalty and after you came back from N.Y. I loved you so terribly—and my one idea was to wipe out the fact I'd been stupid ... As for the rest of our eight years you seemed to have had a pretty rotten time—with my brutishness and I'm sorry—sorry.

Thelma stayed with the "other woman," Henrietta Metcalfe, in the United States, and Djuna stayed on alone in Paris, worn out by years of intense passion, drinking, and heartache. The desperate pleas from Thelma continued to arrive via letter but Djuna had had enough.

I dream of you every night—and sometimes Djuna I dream we are lovers and I wake up the next day and nearly die of shame. Taking advantage in my sleep of something I know so intimately—and something you do not wish me to have. It's like stealing from you and I feel the next day like cabling "forgive me" and sitting up all night ... I'd do anything in the world to please you a little—but what is it I can do? I don't know which foot forward I'm so certain both are wrong.

A desire for revenge, an attempt to exorcise her personal demons, and those magical, inexplicable motives for which writers write, even in their darkest hours, were forces which combined to propel Djuna Barnes into the voracious writing project she engaged in for over eight years, from 1927 to 1935, which eventually became *Nightwood*.

It has been suggested that in the writing of *Nightwood*, and specifically in the creation of Robin, Djuna Barnes conflated her relationship to Thelma with the sexual abuse of her childhood.[12] Djuna wrote to Emily Holmes Coleman, a friend she had met through Peggy Guggenheim, "I am up to my neck here in my lost life — Thelma & Thelma only — & my youth — way back in the beginning when she had no part in it & yet she is the cause of my remembrance of it." Djuna admitted that the character of Robin Vote was modeled on Thelma — which she knew would anger her — but claimed, unconvincingly, that Nora Flood was based on Thelma's lover Henrietta Metcalfe rather than on herself. It was, undeniably, Djuna who followed Thelma in anguish just as Robin followed Nora in *Nightwood*:

> Suffering is the decay of the heart. In the beginning, after
> Robin went away to America, I searched for her in the ports. I
> sought Robin in Marseille, in Tangier, in Naples, to understand
> her, to do away with my terror. I said to myself, I will do what
> she has done, I will love what she has loved, then I will find her
> again. At first it seemed that all I should have to do would be
> to become "debauched," to find the girls that she had loved;
> but I found that they were only girls that she had forgotten. I
> haunted the cafés where Robin had lived her nightlife; I drank
> with the men, I danced with the women, but all I knew was
> that others had slept with my lover.

Ultimately *Nightwood* is much more than a road map to the disintegration of a tortured love affair. It has been considered a visionary allegorical tale of the rising tide of fascism across Europe, in which Jews, homosexuals, and other marginalized outsiders constitute Hitler's degenerate *Untermenschen*. Some have read it as a feminist reworking of Dante's *Divine Comedy*, in which the price paid for personal and sexual freedom is judgment and damnation; others have claimed it is a lesbian rage against the clergy and a "feminist-anarchist call for freedom." The novel is open to such a range of interpretations precisely

because its author was not interested in the "realistic." She claimed to work with her intuition and over the years of rewriting, she transformed her "remembrance of time and pain" into something quite beyond her personal history.

Emily Holmes Coleman served as "midwife" to the novel, nurturing and encouraging Djuna's writing to such an extent that Djuna's mother found such behavior to be not "normal." As the publishers' rejections continued to arrive, Emily, determined to find a publisher at any cost, argued that Djuna should eliminate the story of Felix (the Jew Nora later marries), reduce the story of the Doctor Matthew O'Connor (a transsexual with dubious medical credentials), and stick closely to her central narrative: the tragic relationship between Robin and Nora. Djuna refused, insisting that

> Robin's marriage to Felix *is* necessary to the book for this reason (which you can not know, not having lived with a woman having loved her and yet circulated in public with the public aware of it) that people *always* say, "Well of course those two women would never have been in love with each other if they had been *normal*, if any man had slept with them, if they had been well f——and had born a child." Which is ignorance and utterly false, I married Robin to prove this point, she had married, had had a child yet was still "incurable."

As for the transsexual doctor, he plays an indispensable role as well. Andrew Field argues that Dr. O'Connor is the key to the narrative:

> [The story of *Nightwood*] is the profound and impossible love of a woman who contemplates and understands for a woman who rages and destroys … There is, too, the very great problem of perspective because Dr. O'Connor is both of and not of the main story. Dr. O'Connor is an entire Greek chorus put into a single character, and that character, moreover, stands very near to the reader so that his apparent dimensions are

LEFT: "Djuna was tall, quite handsome, bold-voiced, and a remarkable talker, full of reminiscences of her Washington Square New York life and her eccentric childhood somewhere up the Hudson." —Janet Flanner

much enlarged. Once that is seen, once the painterly trick of perspective is grasped, whereby the main story is moved upstage where it must appear somewhat reduced, then *Nightwood* has a plot.[13]

In late 1931, Djuna was recovering from an appendicitis operation and the American writer Charles Henri Ford moved in with her, which led to a brief, unstable affair (before he moved on to a relationship with the painter Pavel Tchelitchew). But Djuna was restless, sick of Paris and unsure where else to go. To friends she complained that "Montparnasse has ceased to exist. There is nothing left but a big crowd … Montparnasse is all over. And Greenwich Village is all over. It's all all over."[14] Keeping Paris as her base, Djuna moved aimlessly to New York, to Tangier, to Peggy Guggenheim's English country house, where she continued working on *Nightwood,* to London, and back to Paris.

T.S. Eliot, then senior editor at Faber and Faber, is usually credited with rescuing the manuscript of *Nightwood* from its endless, discouraging rounds of publishers' rejections. Sylvia Beach wrote that: "Fortunately, T.S. Eliot, with his usual discernment, sought her out and ushered her to the place she deserves to occupy."[15] But Emily Coleman virtually forced Eliot to take Djuna's manuscript, which he did, despite reservations, while cutting it down by two-thirds its length.

When it was finally published in 1936, *Nightwood* was largely ignored by critics, although it has since achieved a kind of cult status. It received a few terrible reviews, but even the favorable ones did not know what to make of it—calling it "Strange and Brilliant," "Queer, Morbid, and Interesting," "The Twilight of the Abnormal."

It seems odd that Djuna Barnes's lesbian themes were so overtly presented while Gertrude Stein's were so carefully disguised. Yet Gertrude Stein was ridiculed and despised for being a lesbian, whereas Djuna Barnes was respected and accepted

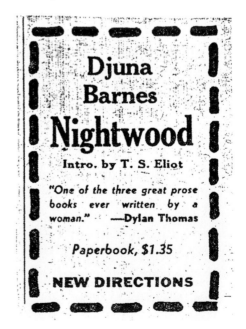

Djuna Barnes

Nightwood

Intro. by T. S. Eliot

"One of the three great prose books ever written by a woman." —Dylan Thomas

Paperbook, $1.35

NEW DIRECTIONS

ABOVE: Djuna Barnes's self-portrait around the time her illnesses began.

within the heterosexual Modernist community. Shari Benstock suggests a reason for this paradox: it was inconceivable "that a woman as beautiful as Barnes might be lesbian" and therefore her lesbian themes were read as "confirmation of the degradation and innate depravity of homosexuality, turning these texts against themselves."[16]

During the mid- to late-1930s, Djuna Barnes was in and out of hospital. Solita Solano recalled that "when in trouble" Djuna would stay with her and Janet Flanner, and on occasion they would have to take her to the American Hospital. She became increasingly quarrelsome and violent, and was considered insane by the staff in the nursing

KILHAM

Lament for the Left Bank
by DJUNA BARNES

PERSONALLY I would give all I have, except what I got from it, to be back in Paris again as it was, sitting at a bistro table with its iron legs in the sawdust from the escargot baskets, the cheap, badly-pressed cotton napkin coming off all over my best cloak—that napkin with its hems always half turned and heavy with the blood-red of yesterday's burgundy—a carafe of vin ordinaire before me, an oval dish of salade de tomate, a bowl of cress soup, a blanquette de veau, green almonds—anything—only to hear again the sad, angry popping of the taxi horns, the gracious flowing language chattered by clerks off for two hours of food and argument. To see the patchwork theatrical placards on the kiosks, the pink-paper lampoons on the plaster wall of the house across the way (these were

ABOVE: During the Occupation of Paris, Djuna wrote this article, a lament for the Paris that was no more.

home where she was recuperating from what was at least her second nervous breakdown. For a time her friends didn't know to where she had disappeared. Just as war was breaking out across Europe, Emily Coleman found her and Peggy Guggenheim provided her boat fare back to New York, even though she doubted that Djuna, frail and penniless, would survive the journey.

In 1939, Djuna Barnes settled in New York. Natalie Barney regretted not getting a chance to say farewell and wrote, "for farewell you must! and not let little love affairs lead to such extremes! Why not go back ... to pull yourself together for the sake of your great gift?"

But Djuna Barnes had no more love affairs, little or large, and not much materialized from her great gift in the following forty-odd years. Having told Robert McAlmon in Paris that "... I might as well go back to Greenwich Village and rot there," that is essentially what she did. Although she still attempted to write, "very slowly, tear everything up, more or less, and start all over again"[17]—she spent the rest of her life bitter and reclusive, addicted to drugs and alcohol, and financially supported by Natalie Barney, Peggy Guggenheim, and, occasionally, Janet Flanner.

In 1943, Peggy Guggenheim's Manhattan gallery ran an exhibition of Djuna Barnes's drawings and paintings, the only public acknowledgement she received for her parallel career as a visual artist. Her years of frustrated writing did produce a last verse drama, *The Antiphon*, published in 1959. But these public events did not lure her out of private seclusion. She never even managed to see her old friend Mina Loy, also back in New York and living an equally reclusive life on the Bowery. Although for decades Djuna Barnes refused interviews and scorned the publication of various memoirs and biographies that romanticized the Paris of old, in her seventies she wrote to Natalie Barney, "of course I think of the past and of Paris, what else is there to remember?"

5

LETTERS FROM PARIS

Janet to Genêt

Janet Flanner's will, written in Paris in 1923, requested that any papers found after her death be destroyed by fire without first being opened or perused, as "one writes down many thoughts and hopes during one's life that seem trivial and unsightly if one is not alive to defend them."

Janet amended her will in later years, and Solita Solano saved most things that Janet was inclined to throw away. When the two women were in their late seventies, Solita donated the lot (minus any reference to their sexual lives) to the Library of Congress, despite a previous letter from Janet to the library that claimed she had nothing of value. It's fortunate for us, because during the many years she was living and working in Paris, Janet Flanner was possibly the single most influential writer on the Left Bank.

Such a pronouncement would greatly surprise Janet Flanner herself, despite her having received the Legion of Honor from the French government in 1947, an honorary doctorate from Smith College in 1958, and many other public honors. In 1964, when she was compiling an anthology of her writings from the twenties and thirties, she still found many of her thoughts trivial and unsightly, and was embarrassed that they had made their way into

LEFT: A portrait of "Genêt of The New Yorker."

print even the first time around. Ever self-doubting, she considered herself "merely" a journalist, not quite a writer.

As the personality behind the pen name "Genêt," Janet Flanner for half a century wrote a fortnightly "Letter from Paris" for publication in *The New Yorker* magazine. In this letter she commented cleverly and often wisely on everything from *haute couture* to the ballet, new music, modern art, and even the rise of fascism. She wrote not as an outside observer but as a participant who experienced firsthand the cultural world around her. Her popular column, read by Americans thirsty for knowledge about Parisian life, became an institution in its own right in which virtually all the artists and writers of the Left Bank are immortalized. Her position as a journalist for a new but increasingly important cultural magazine gave her an entrée to everyone

BELOW: Janet and Solita in Crete in 1921, where Solita wrote travelogues for *National Geographic.*

and everything, and resulted in a privileged overview of life in Paris across the social spectrum.

Janet was strategically placed at the center of the Modernist movement in Paris, yet she was traditional to the point of romanticism: "I wanted beauty, with a capital B. I came to find the art and culture I couldn't find in America."[1] In her *New Yorker* letter she would repeat this barb through her cultural contrasts: "We recall that while America was making candles, Paris was making Voltaire." She might be excused such an insult for she came from the American heartland herself. Born in 1892, she was of solid, middle-class, Midwestern Protestant stock, but despised what she saw as the puritanism, materialism, hypocrisy, and standardization of America. She described, with typical Flanner humor, how her background came in useful for life in France: "My mother's people came from a Quaker

ABOVE: Solita Solano, shortly after she met Janet Flanner.

settlement in Indiana. I was brought up as a semi-Quaker. That's probably why I get along so well in France—I attach an importance to religion, especially if I don't have to practice it ..."[2]

A trip to Europe at the age of seventeen introduced her to "the beauties of Europe, the long accretions of architecture and poetry and civilization and education ..."[3] But it would be some time before she returned to the continent. At 26, she came a step closer: she moved from her home of Indiana to New York City with her new husband, Lane Rehm. Shortly after their arrival, she fell in love with Solita Solano, four years her senior. Janet was struck by Solita's "large swimming eyes of an intense blue."[4]

When the two first met at the end of the First World War, Solita had run away from her husband and was now working as drama critic for the *New York Tribune.* The opportunity to travel together came when Solita was offered an assignment in Constantinople and Crete for *National Geographic;* the two women set off for southern Europe

ABOVE: Janet's watercolor painting of her room in the Hotel Napoléon Bonaparte in Paris.

and the Levant in 1921, hardly a conventional act for "unescorted" middle-class, married American women at that time.

In 1922, Janet and Solita settled in Paris and took two rooms in the extremely narrow Hotel Napoléon Bonaparte, a fourth-floor walk-up in the rue Bonaparte. Solita described its appeal:

> Having given up our jobs, we romantically had little money ...
> The Hotel Napoléon Bonaparte was perfect for our purposes;
> it cost a dollar a day and was near the Seine, the Louvre, and
> the auto buses. Its charms were certainly not in its amenities;
> those we built in ourselves much later ... The top floor was
> important to us all, for next to room 20 was the hotel's unique
> bathroom, barely containing a tub and chair ... Our ideal,
> all-purpose hotel—no domesticity, privacy for work and
> study, all delights free and within walking distance ...[5]

Here they lived together for almost two decades, until France entered the Second World War. The two women remained intimate for the rest of their lives, despite the complications—and there were many —of other partners. Janet chose Paris not only for its art and culture but also to get away from her husband, to whom she felt she had behaved criminally (she felt guilty most of her life for having married him primarily to get out of Indiana). Paris offered her the freedom to live as she wished with Solita.

The pair often appeared in costume at Natalie Barney's afternoon tea parties in the garden, or would be seen sipping cocktails with Djuna Barnes at the Café Flore or lunching with the English heiress Nancy Cunard at their favorite restaurant, La Quatrième République in the rue Jacob. Solita imagined how they must have appeared to others while offering a vivid recollection of what Janet was like at that time:

ABOVE: Janet wrote on the back of this: "Watercolor sketch I did for a wall panel as an illustration of reality, and to be painted by Gene McCowan in a projected flat in Montparnasse which I never took with Solita Solano. This idea was to be a corrective to painters who paint useless portraits of people instead of descriptions of the lives they lead."

> The combined looks of the trio must have been striking: Nancy's Egyptian head with Nefertiti's proud eyes and fine taut mouth painted scarlet ... ; Janet, two years before she was *The New Yorker's* Genêt and still not quite recovered from Henry James and Walter Pater, was magnetically handsome in a way which she claimed could be seen, under the surface of her large intelligent features, that "I'm going to look like Voltaire one day." She was voluble from birth. Painters begged her to stop talking and sit for them ... Janet's hands should be spoken of; they were two small rarities which served but two conscious purposes—two-fingered typing (and at what staccato speeds!) and the maintaining in awkward, practical position the ever-breathing cigarette.[6]

When Janet was not at Natalie Barney's, Café Flore, or La Quatrième République, she was at the Café des Deux Magots. And it was precisely this debauched café life, and the envy it provoked in others, which landed her the job at the *New Yorker.*

ABOVE: Janet Flanner, in front of a portrait of her lifelong friend, Solita Solano.

Back home in New York, her friend Jane Grant loved the witty, newsy, personal letters she received from Janet, and asked Janet to write a biweekly letter for the magazine she and her husband Harold Ross were starting up: "'You need to get to work,' I wrote, for she had declared she was going to loaf at the Deux Magots the rest of her life—maybe write a book when the spirit moved her."[7]

The spirit had already moved her to write one book, *The Cubicle City,* a novel about New York that G.P. Putnam's Sons published in 1925. Solita was even more productive. By the time Janet had begun her *New Yorker* job in 1925, Solita had written two novels, *The Uncertain Feast* (1924) and *The Happy Failure* (1925), and was at work on a third, *This Way Up* (1926). The positive reviews that greeted her first novel give some insight into the double bind in which women writers, trying to be simply "writers," were often trapped, even in the "liberated" twenties. The *Paris Tribune* found that

Although written by a woman, [*The Uncertain Feast*] has not the usual feminine garrulity that makes women writers produce enormous volumes without feeling or insight. Her story is told in sharply chiseled sentences and stark evocations of moods. She has "measure" and analysis. She stands over the corpses of emotions and dissects them without shuddering. To be sure, in the portraiture of women and their enigmatic banalities she is less successful than in the pathological introspection of men's minds and souls. Her women always seem slightly unreal, but when she begins to paint men, she gives us unforgettable impressions of keen understanding.[8]

Despite such backhanded compliments, Solita's novels didn't sell well and she was forced to resume journalism. She also attempted poetry, some of which was published in small magazines or included in her 1934 volume, *Statue in a field,* privately printed in Paris.

Janet's letter for *The New Yorker* not only replaced her own attempts at fiction but soon overshadowed Solita's literary efforts as well. With the creation of "Genêt," Solita's work was henceforth divided between her own writing and her new function as personal editor, sounding board, and literary assistant to Janet, or, as she modestly described herself fifty years later, "Genêt's friend, amateur sec'try and guardian of the thesaurus."[9] Solita later extended her unpaid editorial services to Nancy Cunard, Ernest Hemingway, and Margaret Anderson, and translated into English the poetry of other close friends, such as Colette's protégée, Germaine Beaumont.

Janet had higher regard for fiction, yet her *oeuvre* was really journalism, about which she seemed to be forever apologizing. In her old age, as special guest speaker before the American Institute of Arts and Letters annual meeting in New York, she described herself self-denigratingly:

> I must be the single mere journeyman writer who is a member of this august national institute … I represent the lower class in writing. I am only a reporter. You other writing members are poets, novelists, historians, playwrights, literary critics, commentators on state affairs. In any case, the gentry of writing who write books. I only write columns …[10]

She took to those columns "like a duck takes to water—tentatively at first and then with a wild abandon."[11] She wrote a unique kind of journalism that she hammered out and defined. She would move from the Stavisky fraud scandal to regulations on the price of wheat, from the funeral procession of a French historian specializing in Napóleon to a street scrimmage between teenage Royalists and France's next Prime Minister, Léon Blum, often within the same sentence. Not only did this give her readers a fascinating insight into how her mind worked, it made them feel present at the moment of writing. And although her style had the ease of a clever conversation, she said of it:

> It hasn't always been easy. I'm a nitpicker. Writing, contrary to what a lot of readers think, isn't just a question of knocking out words. The thoughts count just as much. So does the

information and the rhythm ... If something doesn't work, I start again from scratch—using the same thought but new words.[12]

She was a keen observer, but not at all an objective or detached one; objectivity and detachment weren't even professional aspirations. Her personality was in everything she wrote, and became more, not less, pronounced as she gained confidence as a writer. She later wrote,

> This was a new type of journalistic foreign correspondence, which I had to integrate and develop, since there was no antecedent for it. The *New Yorker,* at its beginnings, was also like an oversized minnow learning to swim. It had not yet found its style, and it was to take me some time before I began to find my own, which instinctively leaned toward comments with a critical edge, indeed a double edge, if possible. Criticism, to be valid, in my opinion, demanded a certain personal aspect or slant of the writer's mind.[13]

Her fascinating and at times highly unconventional connections between the arts, fashion, daily life, and the economy ensured for her a respected and continued place in the magazine. Jane Grant remembered that, "Her criticism of art, music, public figures, her coverage of expositions and important events were so expertly handled that her feature was soon influential in the magazine. She had established a new standard, constructed a new mold."[14] At a time when *The New Yorker* featured a regular column, "On and Off the Avenue: Feminine Fashions," and ran large ads for Paris hats ("straight from the Paris openings") at Macy's and Bamberger's department stores, Flanner would slip into her piece on Parisian fashion an unexpected aside on the exploitation of French women workers by the fashion industry. When she wrote about the expatriate experience in France, she was careful to consider the French perspective on Americans in their city, who seemed rich in a country and among a people still struggling under the financial burden of World War I.

The striking contrast between American wealth and French poverty after the war may have moved her to remind her readers of this discrepancy, or perhaps she was only thinking of her editor's admonition. Her sole guideline from *The New Yorker* was to try and get at what the French people thought, rather than focus solely on the opinions of expatriates. Janet frankly did not usually know what the French thought, even if she knew what the French press, which she perused constantly, said. She often wrote about France in her column and elsewhere with sweeping generalizations bordering on stereotype, but as she loved French culture, these generalizations are invariably harmless and usually charming:

> The French are perhaps too civilized as a rule to have much taste for [nature]. They largely think all trees are elms if in parks or willows if by water because Corot painted them like that and made his fortune when his far better art, his early portraits, failed to sell … And certainly the French are not real bird lovers except when the bird is a quail or a pheasant, lying hot on its toasted canape with a watercress salad.[15]

Sometimes she gave up searching for such far-flung explanations and simply admitted to not understanding why the French were so unrelentingly French. She wrote,

> Every country eats well in some ways, in its own opinion and at its own table. But everyone eats better in Paris. And there is no explanation for this … There is no valid explanation why the French, more than anyone else for the past four hundred years … have been uninterruptedly and greatly talented in painting; or why for the same length of time they wrote great literature, or when they did not, at least wrote great French writing, which is, of course, a different thing. These cases of protracted talent in nations are mysteries of the population and parenthood.[16]

As a participant in the French and, especially, expatriate artistic community on the Left Bank, Janet wrote regularly about its activities, and here she was on much more solid ground. As a feminist, she was particularly interested in the accomplishments of women. In 1927, when leading French filmmaker Germaine Dulac began *Schemas*, a new magazine on film and photography, Janet Flanner found it worthy of mention for her American audience. In 1929 she reported on Nancy Cunard's opening of her Hours Press; in 1933 she announced the forthcoming publication of Gertrude Stein's *Autobiography of*

Alice B. Toklas; in 1935 she publicized a sale of manuscripts at Shake-speare and Company, which had fallen on hard times. Similarly she commented on the appearance of new illustrated editions of work by painter Marie Laurencin, the publication in *transition* magazine of sections from Djuna Barnes's forthcoming novel *Ryder,* and the exhibition of Marie Monnier's embroidered tapestries "to rebuke the impatient eye" at her sister Adrienne's bookshop, La Maison des Amis des Livres.

Paris in Black and White

In April 1927, Janet Flanner reviewed an exhibition of photographs by fellow American expatriate Berenice Abbott, at the Sacre du Prin-temps. The exhibit included portraits of leading Modernists, including André Gide, Sylvia Beach, James Joyce, Djuna Barnes, and Jean Coc-teau, which Janet Flanner cryptically called "poetic and brief. The poet himself has been eliminated."

Berenice Abbott had been an independent photographer for two years, having worked for Man Ray as assistant and occasional model. She brought to her photography a background in design, painting, and sculpture, as well as her apprenticeship experience. She had been especially invaluable to Man Ray in the darkroom because she had "this knack for printing. I could feel the space in the print ... I had an uncanny sense about developing prints."[17] But soon she began to take photographs herself on her lunch break; mostly they were portraits of her friends—Thelma Wood, Marie Laurencin, Eileen Gray, and Edna St. Vincent Millay. She was averse to imposing an image on her sub-ject and instead brought out, without romanticizing or analyzing, the image created by her subjects themselves. Janet Flanner was impressed with her Modernist approach: "The frippery of lights, false and stim-ulating, is not Miss Abbot's [sic] genre. Stolidly, as if almost acciden-tally, she arrives at a posturing of her subject so that mind and matter are clothed and balanced against a sensitive plate."

The *Paris Tribune* ran a review of her photographs, further empha-sizing their Modernist qualities:

> She is a skillful worker in black and white, using these two
> extremes with careful precision. She molds and shadows with

ABOVE: Man Ray took this photograph of Berenice Abbott, which she developed.

the experience of an artist and the effects derived are what might be called "camera-drawn studies." In her work is manifested an extreme opposition to all traditional ideas and methods … she finds it necessary to represent her sensitive impression of the person apart from any analysis or study of character. Her portraits are characterized by their broad simplicity and their lack of attention to detail.[18]

For the use of Man Ray's studio during the lunch hour, Berenice Abbott would pay him half of any fees she collected. But her salary was so low that soon she was paying him more than he was paying her, at which point she went into business herself. She was not the

151

only woman to apprentice with Man Ray; the American Lee Miller and the German-born Marianne Breslauer both came to Paris in 1929 and found themselves working in his studio. Marianne Breslauer photographed the city extensively, and made many portraits of artists, including Picasso and Vollard.

When Berenice Abbott and Man Ray parted ways, Bryher gave Berenice her first camera as a gift. Bryher would later write to Sylvia Beach that she "tried always to do what [I] could for the real artists, and especially the woman artist." Berenice Abbott was supported by Bryher in another, more indirect way, which was through Bryher's financial backing of Sylvia Beach's Shakespeare and Company. Not only were Berenice's photographs on permanent exhibition in the bookshop but, as both photographer and poet, she was represented in the little magazines sold in the shop as well. As Shakespeare and Company was the primary outlet for them, as well as the meeting point for their contributors, Sylvia rightly considered herself the "mother" of these journals, which was no small task. For it was, in the words of Bryher, "the moment of glory for the little reviews."[19]

The Little Review

Margaret Anderson began *The Little Review* "because I wanted an intelligent life." What she meant by intelligent was holding creative opinions; what she meant by art was actually ideas about art. Margaret Anderson could not find creative opinions in Indiana in 1912, just as Janet Flanner failed to a few years later. Trained as a pianist, Margaret Anderson was, in the words of Janet Flanner, "the born enemy of convention and discipline—a feminist romantic rebel with an appetite for Chopin and for indiscriminate reading."[20]

Margaret went first to Chicago where she landed a job as a bookshop clerk, earning eight dollars a week. On impulse and a shoestring she started *The Little Review.* Not being one to settle for second best, she was determined it would become the most important magazine in the western world. She knew nothing about publishing, not even

LEFT: Berenice Abbott's well-known portrait of her friend Janet Flanner, wearing the top hat of Nancy Cunard's father.

LEFT: Margaret Anderson

ABOVE: Jane Heap. The buzz and the sting.

"that you had to read proofs when they came from the printer," she later recalled.[21]

The first issue appeared in March 1914, and featured, among other items, a critique of "The Cubist Literature of Gertrude Stein": "… she has eliminated verbs and sentence structure entirely, flinging a succession of image-nouns at the reader. One can surely not accuse her of 'prettiness.'" This was mild stuff compared to the third issue, published in May 1914, which scandalized Chicago by praising the ethics of the anarchist Emma Goldman, who had arrived in town for a lecture.

Margaret thrived on controversy, and launched a subscription campaign to raise funds for the next issue. She had barely enough to eat, and not enough for rent, so she moved, with her sister and her sister's two young sons, and even the volunteer office assistant, to the shores of Lake Michigan. There they staked a tent and began work on the next issue which featured the first in a series on Nietzsche. Margaret later wrote, "Since we were a revolutionary magazine, Nietzsche was naturally our prophet."[22] A group of "revolutionary Nietzschean beachcombers" made good copy for the *Chicago Tribune* and the resulting publicity brought in enough subscriptions to rescue them from tent-living just before the freezing Chicago winter set in.

Margaret Anderson was impressionable and restless, intellectually as well as physically; she was by turns as interested in anarchism, feminism, or psychoanalysis as she was in art. The journal was given a more defined character once Margaret brought on Jane Heap to be the assistant editor. They promptly brought out an issue of 64 blank pages, with the pronouncement that none of the contributions was up to their standards. They were not willing to compromise with the public, having subtitled the journal "A Magazine of the Arts, Making no Compromise with the Public Taste," and likewise would not compromise with mediocre contributors.

Jane Heap was a brilliant woman with a fascinating past. Her father headed a mental asylum in the Midwest, and Jane had grown up among the patients, drawn to the interesting and instructive ways their minds worked.

In the twenties in Paris, the male Modernists, including Ezra Pound and Robert McAlmon, found Jane's overt lesbianism and male cross-dressing threatening. Margaret and Jane must have made a striking pair of contrasts, for Janet Flanner has described Margaret Anderson as "so pretty and feminine a creature." They also perceived their personalities as complementary—in Jane Heap's metaphor, Margaret was the buzz and Jane the sting.

Margaret and Jane and the magazine were, after a brief move to California, now settled in New York. Ezra Pound was appointed as the European editor, a mixed blessing, it seems. He brought with him a small subsidy and a large number of manuscripts by Yeats, T.S. Eliot, Wyndham Lewis, James Joyce, and himself. But at the same time he had "designs" on the vulnerable magazine: "I want an 'official organ'

ABOVE Margaret Anderson and Jane Heap (center, standing) met their foreign editor Ezra Pound (far right, standing) for the first time when they arrived in Paris. They also met Man Ray (with camera), his model Kiki (standing behind him), Modernist poet Mina Loy (kneeling) and filmmaker/poet Jean Cocteau (with cane), among many others.

(vile phrase). I mean I want a place where I and T.S. Eliot can appear once a month … and where Joyce can appear when he likes … *Definitely* a place for our regular appearance …"[23]

The *Paris Tribune* reported that editors Margaret Anderson and Jane Heap had been misguided, confused, and lacking in aesthetic judgment until Ezra Pound "stepped in as European editor and his influence seems to have given *The Little Review* a sort of direction for the time being …"[24] It was pronouncements such as these that enabled history to distort and minimize the contributions of women to the Modernist movement. Indeed the *New York Times Literary Supplement*, reviewing a reissue of *The Little Review* in 1968, could get away with claiming that "Pound was the only participant in *The Little Review* who knew what he was doing and had the executive force to do it."

It was not the first magazine run by women that Ezra Pound had attempted to "influence": he was foreign correspondent for Harriet

Monroe's *Poetry* Magazine, where he published his dogma on Imagism and "introduced" the poet H.D. He subsequently took over the English journal, the *New Freewoman,* which lost its feminist focus and changed its name to *The Egoist* within six months of Pound becoming its literary editor.

Although Pound's "power base" at *The Little Review* enabled it to attract interesting writers, at times his affiliation also worked against them. The poet Amy Lowell felt that "Margaret Anderson has gone over body and soul to Ezra," a charge Margaret forever denied. H.D. found Pound's behavior at *The Little Review* reason enough to stay away, "to keep out of the purlieus." She had been asked by Margaret Anderson to contribute regularly but decided against it on account of Pound's involvement: "Me thinks, for the present, we will keep entirely out."[25]

James Joyce, however, wanted entirely in, and his epic *Ulysses* came out in 23 monthly installments between 1918 and 1920 in *The Little Review.* The U.S. Post Office put the torch to three issues it deemed obscene, which Margaret felt was

> like a burning at the stake, as far as I was concerned. The care
> we had taken to preserve Joyce's text intact; the worry over the
> bills that accumulated when we had no advance funds; the
> technique I used on printer, bookbinder, paper houses—tears,
> prayers, hysterics, or rages—to make them push ahead without
> a guarantee of money; the addressing, wrapping, stamping,
> mailing; the excitement of anticipating the world's response to
> the literary masterpiece of our generation ... and then a notice
> from the Post Office: BURNED.[26]

That, however, was not the end of the saga. The Committee for the Suppression of Vice, headed by a Mr. Sumner, issued an injunction against the magazine on the grounds of obscenity and the women were dragged into court. Their lawyer and short-term benefactor, John Quinn, represented them in the lost cause. Or more accurately, he represented James Joyce and his literary merits, neither of which was on trial, because he felt the two women were "damned fools" without "an ounce of sense" for even attempting the publication of *Ulysses* in the first place. Janet Flanner later recalled that not a single newspaper printed a defense of either James Joyce or his senseless editors, for fear of being associated with the scandal. The *Paris Tribune* questioned whether Margaret Anderson and Jane Heap "ever really understood" *Ulysses,* despite the ordeal its publication put them through. A high point in the proceedings must have been when one of the three elderly male judges assumed a chivalrous, protective attitude toward Margaret and wouldn't allow the offending passages of the novel to be read aloud in her presence—as if she had never read them herself.

Jane Heap and Margaret Anderson were fingerprinted and the magazine was fined $100. It is possible they would have fared better had Jane represented them herself, for she certainly had a persuasive way with words. On the matter of obscenity and its headmaster, Mr. Sumner, she wrote: "It was the poet, the artist, who discovered love, created the lover, made sex everything that it is beyond a function. It is the Mr. Sumners who have made it an obscenity."

Undefeated, the persistent team moved on to the less puritanical city of Paris in 1923 and carried on publishing. Francis Picabia had become their French editor the year before, but that caused no conflict since, according to Margaret, "We had never had anything from him except a Picabia number."[27] Margaret and Jane had found and printed leading French avant-garde writers without Picabia's help, and would continue to do so.

Ezra Pound no longer served as foreign editor; most accounts simply reported that a base in Paris alleviated the need for a European editor. But perhaps the editors, finally encountering him in person, also hastened his departure. After their first meeting, when he was 38 years old, Margaret commented that "it will be more interesting to know him when he has grown up."[28]

Margaret Anderson soon left *The Little Review* as well, but without removing her own name from the masthead. It was not the court case, the financial penalty, the negative publicity, the obscene hate letters she received, or even her impoverished existence that made her finally give it up. It was simply that she had found something new which commanded all her attention: an actress and singer named Georgette LeBlanc, who for twenty years had been the on- and offstage leading lady for the Belgian poet and playwright, Maurice Maeterlinck.

Janet Flanner recalled, "From the first, [the two women] formed an attachment with all the signs of permanence."[29] The signs weren't wrong: they turned out to be inseparable until Georgette's slow, painful death from cancer twenty years later. Her *Herald Tribune* obituary in 1941 suggests Georgette had a hand in Maeterlinck's perceived genius:

> Her influence on the life and work of the Belgian poet was concededly profound. In recent years, since Maeterlinck's pen has been inactive, there has been conjecture as to whether it was the break with Mme LeBlanc that was responsible for the dimming of a talent that for thirty years had burned so brightly.

Apparently Georgette LeBlanc's own talents did not dim with the break from Maeterlinck. She continued to give concerts and poetry recitals in New York and Paris that, according to Janet Flanner, "literally moved her listeners to tears." For Janet, who despised Georgette's music, they might have been tears of misery, but she ignored her personal dislike and duly clarified the weepy response of Georgette's devoted audience: "tears of pleasure, tears of tenderness." Relying on her early professional music training, Margaret accompanied Georgette on the piano.

Whether or not Georgette LeBlanc and her piano accompanist were paid for these recitals Janet does not report, but somehow the two were no better off financially than when Margaret carried the burden of *The Little Review.* More astonishingly, their poverty did not seem to cramp their lifestyle. When Margaret wrote her memoirs, an entire volume of which she devoted to chronicling her intimate friendship with Georgette LeBlanc, she recalled, "At this time we had less money than anyone in the world (including those who have none at all), but we spent twenty years in five of the more celestial French chateaux."

The first of these chateaux was owned by Georgette LeBlanc's sister and her husband, and the stories Margaret Anderson told about her life there with Georgette as unpaying and unwanted family boarders would make any sane person get a job and move into humbler quarters within an hour. Instead, Georgette wrote poetry and they both became devotees—and eventually proselytizers—of the Russo-Greek mystic Georges Gurdjieff whom they had met in the early twenties. Margaret and Georgette lived intermittently for several years at Gurdjieff's chateau retreat, which counted for another of their French celestial homes. Among their successful converts to his doctrine were Jane Heap and Solita Solano. The ever-cynical Janet Flanner was never

LEFT: Djuna Barnes's sketch of singer Georgette LeBlanc.

RIGHT: Jane Heap, a formidable personality who took over the running of *The Little Review.*

susceptible. Meanwhile, Jane Heap continued on until 1929 as the sole working editor of *The Little Review.* No longer an "official organ" for Pound, its scope broadened. It successfully avoided aligning itself with the various warring factions in the art world while giving space to many of them. Margaret Anderson felt relieved that the magazine was in Jane Heap's capable hands. For her, Jane was "the most interesting thing that had happened to *The Little Review.* To me the expression, the formulation, of her thoughts amounted to genius."[30]

Jane Heap used her position to help writers she believed in, and to introduce their work to editors and publishers. In particular, she was virtually the self-appointed literary agent for Gertrude Stein. In 1924, she brought Gertrude's writings to the attention of T.S. Eliot, then at *The Criterion,* an English quarterly. Having read nothing of Gertrude's writings despite her enormous output during the previous fifteen years, he was grateful to Jane for landing a manuscript on his desk. Within a year T.S. Eliot had agreed to publication and wrote to Gertrude, "I am immensely interested in everything you write."[31]

Many letters passed between Jane Heap and Gertrude Stein between 1923 and 1928 in which personal expressions of friendship were intermingled with business and professional concerns. In 1925, Jane Heap was deeply involved in selling Gertrude's epic, *The Making of Americans,* to an American publisher. She first tried to retrieve the original

ABOVE: Jane Heap and Margaret Anderson became disillusioned with art, but here they are (last two on right) in the studio of the sculptor Brancusi (far left) with Dadaist Tristan Tzara, an unidentified woman, and poet Mina Loy.

material and rights from publisher Bob McAlmon for $1000 that she didn't have and he surely didn't need. Jane wrote to Gertrude, "I'll get 3 Lives reprinted as well … God—how I have planned and worked for this—I hope it will go through."

But it proved impossible, chiefly because of McAlmon's increasing paranoia. Jane reported a year later on why it hadn't moved forward: "I have seen Bob several times, always drunk. When I talked to him about the book he cursed and said he knows nothing about it—… I had a short talk with Sylvia—Bob has told her that you are cheating him or trying to cheat him."

For her pains, Jane was rewarded with "J.H. Jane Heap" which Gertrude wrote in 1928:

> Jane was her name and Jane her station and Jane her nation and Jane her situation. Thank you for thinking of how do you do how do you like your two percent. Thank you for thinking how do you do thank you Jane thank you too thank you for thinking thank you for thank you. Thank you how do you. Thank you Jane thank you how do you do. An appreciation of Jane.

Gertrude wanted to write a further tribute to Jane Heap for the final issue of *The Little Review* in 1929, but Jane and Margaret (back as coeditor for the grand finale) wanted her instead to answer the questionnaire they had put to all their former contributors. The magazine folded in 1929 in part because it felt it had achieved what it set out to do: to be a voice for the renaissance in the arts which began before the First World War.

But rather than celebrate their success, the editors ended on a disappointed note. Interested not so much in art as in ideas about art, Margaret Anderson felt that "even the artist doesn't know what he is talking about. And I can no longer go on publishing a magazine in which no one really knows what he is talking about. It doesn't interest me." Jane Heap was more damning of the art than the artists, who were not to blame. Rather it was the times in which they lived: "No doubt all so-called thinking people hoped for a new order after the war. This hope was linked with the fallacy that men learn from experience. Facts prove that we learn no more from experience than from our dreams." Her grim comments on human nature complement an equally grim assessment of the review's history: "We have given space in *The Little Review* to 23 new systems of art (all nearly dead), representing 19 countries. In all of this we have not brought forward anything approaching a masterpiece ..."

More than of the times they lived in or of the artists themselves, Jane and Margaret were unjustly critical of the work they themselves had done. They had survived fifteen years of financial, legal, and artistic obstacles to publish the work of unknown writers and artists, many of whom became world-renowned. In Janet Flanner's *New Yorker* column which, after all, was read by a much larger and more mainstream public, Janet regularly reminded her readers that the work of Max Ernst and many others who were now "newsworthy" was first seen in New York in the pages of *The Little Review.*

Jane Heap didn't care, however, about which work subsequently became famous; she cared only about whether it was a masterpiece, and that question she answered invariably in the negative. Even *Ulysses,* for which the magazine is remembered (if remembered at all), she found "too personal, too tortured, too special a document to be a masterpiece in the true sense of the word."

Personal and tortured perhaps, but *Ulysses* eventually became a classic. In the beginning it met with indifference, if not hostility, from *The Little Review* readers. According to Janet Flanner, it was years later, after Sylvia Beach had published *Ulysses* in book form, that Americans began smuggling a contraband copy along with their contraband liquor when they returned from Paris. "At first, it must be admitted, the only motive was the titillation of owning something rare and illegal," Janet recalled, and it was only later that "there was an increasing awareness of the importance of *Ulysses* as literature."[32]

The large body of work by women that appeared in the pages of *The Little Review* and other small magazines did not have the notoriety of *Ulysses* and therefore did not survive in print long enough to stand a chance of being discovered "as literature." Solita Solano, Mina Loy, Bryher, Djuna Barnes, and many other women who were regularly published in the little magazines and small presses have been largely forgotten today, as Joyce's *Ulysses* might easily have been had it not attracted notice for other reasons. Solita Solano's fiction, now long forgotten, was favorably reviewed in its time, although even then a comparison with James Joyce was inevitable: "Miss Solano is the poet of emotional crises. Over her book hovers the phenomenon of *Ulysses.* But she has forged her own style ... kinetic ... tremendously evocative of New York ... the rush of the subway is in every ideation of her heroes and heroines."[33]

Thirty years after the demise of *The Little Review,* Bryher looked through a stack of journals with faded covers and plenty of misprints, and found that they still "blazed with vitality." She reflected that "there were the now famous names beside those of whom nothing more was heard" without stating the obvious: with the sole exception of Gertrude Stein it was the male names which had become famous.[34] Mina Loy, for example, was an important Modernist poet who has been totally forgotten. Perhaps because she wrote a feminist manifesto calling for women to "leave off looking to men to find out what you are not—seek within yourselves to find out what you are," she rarely receives a single mention in memoirs and chronicles of the period, unless it is for her great beauty, or even the beauty of her daughters. Yet e.e. cummings, who emulated her innovative use of spacing and broken lines, while applying them to ridiculing petty, superficial ladies or detailing his encounters with prostitutes, is read today by students everywhere. Although history has, for the most part, passed these women's writings by, they were as important in their day as the works of Ernest Hemingway, James Joyce, Ezra Pound, and e.e. cummings—all of them known only by a small group of dedicated Modernists and read only within the pages of innovative, avant-garde little magazines.

Close-Up and Farther Away

Not all the little magazines were based in Paris, and not all were published by women, but both as contributors and publishers women figured significantly in the little magazine and small press movement. After Pound was dismissed from *The Little Review*, he, together with Ford Madox Ford and Ernest Hemingway, attempted to publish the short-lived *Transatlantic Review*, but it collapsed within a year. Eugene Jolas and Elliot Paul, and later Jolas and his wife Maria, ran the far more successful *transition*, which published the work of many women writers. The Black Sun Press was established in 1924 by the upper-class Bostonian Harry Crosby and his wife, Polly Jacob, who called herself Caresse. In 1929 Harry shot himself in what was apparently a suicide pact with another woman. Caresse carried on the small press work alone, printing beautiful editions of Hemingway, William Faulkner, Kay Boyle, Max Ernst, Carl Jung, George Grosz, and Dorothy Parker.

Bryher and H.D. were each involved in editing a little magazine at one time from outside Paris; H.D. "sub-edited" *The Egoist* from London in 1916 and, a decade later, Bryher began *Close-Up* from her home in Switzerland, but the two must be counted among the Left Bank literary community because of their elaborate ties to Paris.

Bryher's position as coeditor, with Kenneth Macpherson, of *Close-Up: An International Magazine Devoted to Film Art*, was the starting point for many of her closest friendships in Paris. The magazine's subtitle was loosely interpreted, and there was always room for poetry by H.D. or stories by Gertrude Stein. Her first letters to Gertrude began rather formally:

> I have always, from the time I read "Three Lives" and met you, valued your opinion very highly. And I look forward to seeing you again, in the autumn.
>
> Your manuscript arrived this morning and excited us both. It

ABOVE: Gertrude was always annoyed at Margaret Anderson for not paying *The Little Review's* writers, but Bryher made sure Gertrude was paid for her contributions to *Close-Up*.

is one of the finest things you have done, I feel. There is a great feeling of depth and continuity about it, like a short but perfect novel.

Gertrude was impressed with the first two issues of *Close-Up* and was glad to be associated with it. Over the following years she and Alice invited H.D. and Bryher many times to their country house in Bilignin or to come and see them "at any hour" in Paris. Although Gertrude and H.D. were embarked on very different literary endeavors, they exchanged books and, in letters to Bryher, Gertrude wrote favorably about H.D.'s writings. Bryher's closest friend in Paris was Sylvia Beach, who was of course the main, perhaps only, salesperson for *Close-Up* in Paris. But even if she hadn't been, Bryher never passed through Paris without spending time with Sylvia and Adrienne. It is in her private letters to Sylvia that the reasons for her and H.D.'s frequent distance from Paris become clear, from Bryher's perspective at least.

H.D. and Bryher each had histories with men who were extremely well-known and relatively influential among expatriates on the Left Bank and this was reason enough for H.D. and Bryher to stay away. Ezra Pound had known H.D. since 1901 when she was 16; they had been engaged to be married and subsequently involved in a tortured romantic triangle while in the United States. Pound considered H.D.

his protégée, whose poetry he "corrected" in the tearoom of the British Museum before naming her "H.D. lmagiste" by scrawling it at the bottom of her page. The long, complicated relationship with Pound ended when H.D. married Richard Aldington in 1913, but they remained in close contact until H.D.'s death. It is not clear whether she told Pound about her true feelings for Bryher, whom Pound never liked, for H.D. shrugged off a romantic attachment. In one letter to him, she hinted that her relationship with Bryher was merely repayment for child care services: "Br. looked after Perdita [H.D.'s daughter] and as that seemed to be the only thing I was hanging on for … I looked after Br. Of course, this is all very bald … but I am tired of mincing matters and 'pretending'."[35] It is possible that H.D. similarly downplayed her feelings for Pound to Bryher.

Bryher was attempting to divorce Robert McAlmon, who was well-known if not well-liked among writers and bartenders in Paris. Despite his own failure as a writer, he derived status by being the sole publisher on the Left Bank who didn't have to worry about financial risk, and also by being the only person James Joyce could always rely on to pay his bar tab. Both H.D. and Bryher were disturbed by the amount of drinking that went on around Bob McAlmon and "the Bunch," as their friends in Paris were called; for this reason they tended to avoid the city altogether. In retaliation, McAlmon would call Bryher "a frightened rabbit" who wasn't tough enough "to 'take' Paris," which Bryher claimed was untrue. H.D. also felt that she was out of place in fashionable Parisian gatherings. She wrote to Bryher, explaining her reluctance to join her in Paris:

> (April 28, 1924) Now my dear child, don't worry. You know I love you and if I said I wanted you to go alone with the French crowd, it was only that you are young and sweet and I feel I am not elegant and enough up-to-date! But I will try not to be sly and silly. It is only that I feel démodé with elegant people.

When H.D. was in Paris a few years later without Bryher, she enjoyed being at the center of the literary scene, to which she was introduced by Sylvia Beach and Ezra Pound. She wrote to Bryher in Switzerland, "I do, do miss you but had no idea, I could so enjoy Paris." She especially "clicked" on this trip with poet and publisher Nancy Cunard, whom she had never much liked before. She described a typical day in Paris to Bryher, whom she addressed as "Darlingest Fido":

> I went out ... and got a really charming lunch at a new place I have found very much in the open opposite the Luxembourg Gardens Medici fountain. That is nice ... I mean finding these places where really one would know Fido would be content with the food and everything. I had the half of a half a bottle of very delicious wine, I will give Dog too when he comes ... wrote about 20 cards, coffee and smoked while Sorbonne students and art students trailed past and a boy played the violin ... It appears that the Paris better-sort group is pro Hilda Aldington now [H.D.], I suppose the sheer underworld is pro Arabella [Richard Aldington's new wife], anyhow it is funny to be "in" it again ...

Bryher (BELOW) was completely devoted to H.D. (RIGHT), both the woman and the poet.

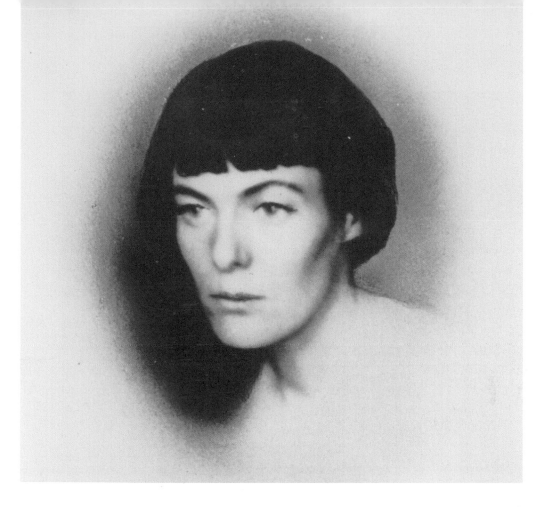

The husbands made things particularly uncomfortable for H.D. and Bryher at times, and given the biases of English law they were difficult to divorce. Bryher explained to Sylvia Beach,

> H.D. would have long ago divorced Aldington had the pro-
> ceedings been in any way decent or possible ... I could get the
> marriage [to Robert McAlmon] annulled on the grounds of
> technical virginity. I don't want to bring up a lot of medical
> details but shall be forced to, if R. to whom I have been consis-
> tently decent, does not do his share of getting the papers
> through.

When the divorce finally did go through, on the grounds of deser-
tion, it meant Bryher could not be seen in Paris very often. She wrote
to Sylvia on 27 March 1927, "As I am 'deserting' R. it is judged better
for me not to be around too much ..." That same year, she confided in
Sylvia the financial payoff he was to receive:

My father is buying back the securities settled on him, which should give him a capital of about fifteen thousand dollars and he will get his allowance up to the end of this year ... This is of course in confidence. I have not heard of or from him lately, except for a short business letter.

Bryher had married McAlmon in order to be left alone by her enormously wealthy family and to be free to travel with H.D. When the divorce went through, she made a far more sensible, although initially equally complicated, choice for her second marriage: her good friend and H.D.'s lover, the Scottish editor and filmmaker, Kenneth Macpherson. In addition to appeasing Bryher's family, the marriage shielded H.D. and Macpherson's affair from H.D.'s husband Richard Aldington. Through Bryher and H.D., Macpherson met the writer Norman Douglas, with whom he would live for many years in Capri.

Bryher and Kenneth Macpherson began *Close-Up* from the village of Territet in Switzerland, where she had moved for tax purposes. There, in 1930, they built a Bauhaus villa on the shores of Lake Geneva where Bryher lived, occasionally with Macpherson and intermittently with H.D. throughout the next decade.

The magazine was the first ever devoted to the *art* of film, which Macpherson emphasized was indeed an art form: "People are still apt to sneer when you talk of films being art ... It has been a film industry, film industry .... But we are going to talk film art at them until the right balance is established." Apparently people were ready to listen, because the initial printing of 500 copies an issue sold out and had to be expanded to 5000 at a time when other little magazines didn't reach outside their small but loyal following.

Through Macpherson, Bryher and H.D. became interested in film aesthetics and in filmmaking as well. Together they produced several short films and one "underground" style feature called *Borderline* which starred H.D., Bryher, and Paul Robeson. But Bryher came to feel that the visual power of film competed with her own creative powers as a writer. She eventually lost interest, especially with the increased use of sound in the 1930s, which to her mind destroyed the cinema's

LEFT: Bryher was tough enough to "take Paris," but preferred the shores of Cornwall, where she first met H.D., and the isles of Scilly, from which she took her name.

development and turned it into "the art that died," as she called it. They ceased publishing *Close-Up* in 1933, due largely to the introduction of sound film.

Bryher used her inherited wealth to endow other marginal artistic and literary projects as well. She generously supported Shakespeare and Company until its closure, at which point she sent personal checks directly to Sylvia. Although she wrote a number of books herself, primarily historical novels and works about education, Bryher's foremost literary priority throughout her life was the support and promotion of H.D.'s creative genius. As Alice did for Gertrude, and Solita did for Janet, so Bryher did for H.D.—she spared no expense or personal sacrifice to ensure that H.D. was always free to write.

Another British woman who used her family's great wealth to underwrite literary endeavors was Nancy Cunard. Knowing nothing whatsoever about printing, she established The Hours Press at her country house in Normandy in the spring of 1928, an event which Janet Flanner publicized in *The New Yorker* as "an item of exceptional interest to New York bibliophiles." The *Paris Tribune* also found Nancy's activities noteworthy, and ran a long article with a comparably long title: "Nancy, the Last of the Famous Cunarders, Steers Her Hand Press into the Stormy Literary Seas of the Montparnasse Surrealists."

The initial publication list included *Canto* by Ezra Pound, *A Plaquette of Poems* by Iris Tree, *The Eaten Heart* by Richard Aldington, and a French translation by Louis Aragon of Lewis Carroll's *The Hunting of the Snark,* all in limited, signed editions. Nancy used a Belgian hand press with eighteenth-century type, and loved the smell of printer's ink, the feel of different paper stock, and the physical and aesthetic work of making beautiful books. According to the *Paris Tribune* announcement,

> Miss Cunard had decided that certain writings by moderns looked better in books than in manuscripts. So she bought a printing press and went to work ... She had ideas about printing, in regard to type, size and form which no one seems to

LEFT: The aristocratic Englishwoman Nancy Cunard, granddaughter of the founder of the famous Cunard steamship company.

To the friends of 1
from
the friend of 2.
= your loving Nancy
1927/as before and since.

Nancy Cunard

know where she learned. No doubt, they just came to her, as she herself did to the print shop.[36]

Nancy was one of the few heterosexual women in her tight-knit group of female friends in Paris. Bryher recalled that she was so stunning that all heads turned when she walked into a room, and even the *Paris Tribune* reported that, "The pulse of the Inner Circle of Montparnasse is beating much faster now," since Nancy Cunard returned to the Left Bank from her country house in Normandy.

Through her relationships with men she was drawn into various campaigns and causes; her romance with French poet Louis Aragon involved her, briefly and uneasily, in the otherwise largely male Surrealist literary movement. Her subsequent, seven-year off-and-on relationship with Henry Crowder, an African American jazz musician in Paris, not only scandalized her upper-crust English family but introduced her to the "Afro-American cause," as she called it, which changed her life and started her on a path of occasionally misguided but always passionate and dedicated political activism.

Nancy's greatest literary achievement was the compiling, editing, and designing of the unprecedented anthology *Negro,* published in 1934, which consisted of 855 pages, 550 illustrations, and some 150 contributors, two-thirds of whom were black, from three continents. Her greatest lost cause was the Spanish Civil War, to which she gave herself body and soul. Indeed, she never fully accepted that the war *had* been lost, no doubt either a contributing symptom or a manifestation of her later loss of sanity.

Janet's "Paris Letter" profile of Nancy was written long before her descent into alcoholism and madness, when Janet could still simply describe her as

> one of England's best, if most infrequent, poets ... Miss
> Cunard has long been an intransigent hub of modern literary
> interests, has a small and severe collection of great modern
> paintings and an enormous collection of African art, is still
> beautiful, a tireless traveler and a remarkable letter-writer.

LEFT: Solita, Janet, and Nancy were considered a "fixed triangle," which Nancy alluded to when she signed this photo to Janet and Solita.

Friendships and Hostilities

Among the American, British, German and French women in the Modernist community in Paris, there were bound to be close friendships—and equally passionate animosities. Nancy Cunard, Solita Solano, and Janet Flanner formed an exceptionally close-knit family which functioned for each of them as a surrogate blood-tie for the rest of their lives. Solita described them as "a fixed triangle" which "survived all the spring quarrels and the sea changes of forty-two years of modern female fidelity ..."[37] On the other hand, Margaret Anderson and Gertrude Stein quarreled from mutual disdain; in fact, they despised each other. In *The Autobiography of Alice B. Toklas*, Gertrude admitted that "Gertrude Stein then and always liked Jane Heap immensely, Margaret Anderson interested her much less." Djuna Barnes also wasn't particularly keen on Margaret Anderson, whom she didn't respect, or on Gertrude Stein either, for that matter, who "had to be the center of everything. A monstrous ego."[38] In virtually any group, whatever the constellation, Janet Flanner seemed to be on good terms with everyone, and it was her wide network of friends that served to link small clusters of women together into a "community." Even Djuna Barnes, who could be particularly acerbic, wrote affectionately to her "dearest Jannie."

Margaret Anderson tried to hide her immense dislike of Gertrude Stein from Janet, knowing how close the two were. She wrote the following letter, perhaps to get her annoyance about Gertrude out of her system, but refrained from mailing it to Janet:

> Gertrude and I never changed our minds about one another ...
> I knew we could never be friends. There was something so
> *hearty* in her, and so much authority involved in the heartiness.
> She and Jane [Heap] "got on" marvelously, but then Jane could
> be hearty when necessary. I can't, and I can think of no one
> whose heartiness, combined with such serious self-love and
> intensity, could repel me as much as Gertrude's ... My

RIGHT: Djuna Barnes was a sharp dresser with a sharp tongue.

reactions to her were like my reactions to certain music—
"Please don't play it in my hearing, I can't bear it."

An interesting metaphor for Margaret to choose, for her beloved Georgette's singing had the same effect on Janet: it made her "want to jump into the Seine."[39]

But hiding the letter hardly meant hiding its contents, particularly from such a perceptive woman as Janet Flanner. Janet had her own misgivings about both Margaret (her "mysticism" and lack of common sense) and Gertrude (her writings, which she often claimed not to understand), but she managed to keep such differences from overshadowing her genuine devotion to each. After their deaths, she even wrote about the animosity between Margaret and Gertrude in her *New Yorker* column, although she kept herself well out of it.

> Probably it was inevitable that Gertrude and Margaret would not get along, since both were outstanding egotists. Quite often, they would meet in a country house in Orgeval, outside Paris, invited by a mutual friend for Sunday lunch. In such meetings, it was Gertrude's psychology that dominated. Gertrude talked only when she had something to say of definite interest—to herself, and thus, by extension, to her listeners, because she was intelligent and a splendid talker. Her nature was so solid that it reduced Margaret to the two opposite elements always the uppermost in her own personality —violent agreement and violent disagreement ... The Orgeval lunches invariably developed, by the second cups of coffee which ended them, into small verbal wars. These were Margaret's particular delight, and if she was able to say, as she drew on her topcoat to go home, that she'd never had better conversation, it was her way of acknowledging that she had been involved in battles with almost everyone at the table and felt that she had triumphed in most of them.

The Orgeval gatherings were held at the home of Noel Murphy, another American woman who had been drawn to France. Noel was a singer with whom Janet fell passionately in love, an event that did not demand much change in her undomesticated domestic arrangements with Solita. Janet still shared the hotel rooms with Solita in Paris, and she and Solita retreated separately to the countryside of Orgeval—Janet to Noel Murphy, and Solita to someone else she had met, Libby Jenks Clark. Their relationship, committed as ever, opened up to accommodate new loves.

Janet started spending as much time in Orgeval as in Paris (Solita joked in 1932 that Janet "lives with me when she remembers it"[40]) to be with Noel but also to answer her growing need for a retreat from the pressures and demands of work. In the idyllic setting of Orgeval she could think and have time to write. Janet's job remained the same in form only as the twenties gave way to the thirties.

Unlike the vast majority of male expatriates who packed up and repatriated from whence they came as rapidly as the pound or dollar fell against the franc, Gertrude Stein, Janet Flanner, Margaret Anderson, Nancy Cunard, Eileen Gray, Sylvia Beach, Djuna Barnes, Natalie Barney, and most of the other expatriate women remained in France. They had no desire to leave and no place other than Paris that they could call home. The photog-

rapher Berenice Abbott was one of the few who left; returning to New York, she documented its decline during the worst years of the Great Depression.

But for those who stayed on in France, their leisurely arguments over Sunday lunch in the garden in Orgeval would soon become an impossible luxury: before the decade was out they would gather instead to huddle around the radio for news bulletins, wondering what might happen, what to do, and where to go.

While Gertrude and Janet and

RIGHT: Solita Solano was one of the many American women who stayed in Paris long after the stock market crashed and the "tourists" had gone home.

179

other friends were still lunching in the garden, Bryher had already begun using her base in Switzerland and her vast family funds to help Jewish and anti-fascist refugees escape from Germany. The first few refugees showed up in 1933, but by 1934 the exodus had grown drastically. Bryher had been in Berlin in 1932 and was horrified by the tense atmosphere and violence of the Nazis' coming to power. She believed the firsthand stories of the many refugees who came across the border, accounts far bleaker than those in the newspapers. She tried to alert journalists and politicians in other European countries, but met with insult or ridicule.

Nancy Cunard also became involved in the fight against fascism although on France's western rather than eastern border. She wrote continuously from Spain for numerous publications, the most respected of which was the *Manchester Guardian,* condemning the British and French governments for their lack of support for the Spanish republic. She reported passionately on the plight of Spanish refugees, started fundraising drives in England, and donated her own money to help refugees escape into France.

Janet also shifted her priorities from literature and art to politics in the thirties. She was not a correspondent from the front line; her strengths lay more in commentary than reportage. She did eventually go to the Spanish border as refugees were teeming across it, and to Nazi-controlled Austria—for a vacation, oddly enough—but found "history looks queer when you're standing close to it." Her more comfortable approach was to read, cull, synthesize, and analyze European news for the American public, although she was frustrated that with events occurring so quickly her news was often history by the time it reached her readers.

Janet commented with typical sarcasm on the news of the 1929 stock market crash reaching Paris—"at the Ritz bar the pretty ladies are having to pay for their cocktails themselves." But with the departure of the American tourists who had always been good for target practice, coupled with the alarming European political events of the early thirties, Janet's style became less flippant and casual, more serious and urgent. Jane Grant at *The New Yorker* recalled, "In 1930 she

LEFT: The beautiful American singer, Noel Murphy, with whom Janet was smitten.

ABOVE: In the 1930s, Janet retreated to Noel's house in Orgeval to write and relax.

casually carried a paragraph about politics. No comment or criticism from Ross [the editor]. She became bolder. She began to analyze the complex French political scene prior to World War II, with observations both sharp and authoritative."[41]

In "All Gaul is Divided," a brilliant essay written in September 1939 at Noel's house in Orgeval, Janet explained why she had shifted her interests from art to politics; why she felt it inappropriate to write about the arts when the world was in such crisis:

> The arts are peace products. Paris was at peace [in the twenties] and its arts flourished … Certainly when men are frightened of having their bodies dismembered in a war is no moment to inquire, as they start running for cannons, "Are you still fond of Picasso's blue period" or "Do you think Proust's works so bourgeois that they cannot survive?"

Janet was not by nature a radical, nor did she, initially, hold strong political views beyond a passion for justice. Yet she pushed herself to become an authority on European politics as dangerous economic and political forces battled their way through the thirties, and she was radicalized in the process. Although she despaired of her own ignorance, the breadth of her knowledge from which she culled her references, and the sharpness of her mind which produced clever, often brilliant, associations, made Janet Flanner more than a "mere" journalist. Rather, she was the confident, intelligent voice of her generation.

Like the rest of that generation, however, she was slow to realize the extent to which the Nazis were becoming a genuine threat to western civilization. Her profile of Hitler in 1936 comments on his penchants for music and picnic lunches, his unphotogenic appearance and the physical acrobatics required by the "Heil Hitler" salute. Her tone was politically noncommittal, portraying him as pathetic and foolish rather than dangerous.

ABOVE: As a war correspondent, Janet Flanner sometimes felt as though she were writing fiction.

When Berlin put on its best face for the 1936 Olympic Games, Janet went with Noel Murphy to cover it for *The New Yorker.* The massive propaganda strategy behind the Olympics was successful, and Janet, like many other foreign visitors, was impressed with the dazzling pageantry and German organizational skills. She reported on forthcoming changes anticipated in Germany, among them an undertaking she didn't find unreasonable: "a redistribution of real estate, now valuable for the first time since the inflation, and, in Berlin especially, still owned by non-Aryans." Finding the Nazi regime now into its "adult stride," she seemed to miss the ominous meaning behind her own words: "Only a determined deaf-and-blind visitor to any corner of this land could fail to see and hear the sight, the sound, of Germany's forward march."

But the vast majority of the world did fail to see and hear. Bryher herself took evidence to the government and the press in England that, with the one exception of the *Manchester Guardian,* would invariably dismiss it on the grounds of it being too controversial or against the government's policy with Germany at the time. In fact, she would often use copies of *The Times* to hide documents she was smuggling into Germany for refugee visas, so pro-Nazi was the newspaper that the German officials rarely bothered anyone carrying it into the country. Bryher felt sure that the Nazi regime would have collapsed in its infancy had Europe responded swiftly and strongly to its persecution of its own people. Because it hadn't, she remained ashamed of her country for the rest of her life.

As if to justify her own lack of foresight, Janet Flanner later looked back from the brink of war in France to discern how the grim situation

ABOVE: Over the years, Janet slowly developed into the confident, intelligent voice of her generation.

had come about under everyone's eyes:

> The scene did not really grow grave until the middle of the 1930's. The acts of transition that led to the change were various, slow, insensible, incredible, and in no special instance, except by a morbid fortune teller, could their eventually rapid melodramatic outcome have been foretold. Indeed much of what has happened to Europe in the past five years looks as if it had been seen darkly through a glass and by a complicated Cassandra.

If Janet was not a morbid fortune-teller, she did at least see the present moment as clearly as just about anyone, and for the most part her interpretation was right on target. She may have been slow in waking up to the Nazi threat, but when she did, she was fully alert. According to Shari Benstock,

> That her perceptions of the moment still agree with history's assessment of this era suggests a *déjà vu* effect, as though her commentaries derived their impetus from a later perspective.

History has rarely proven her wrong in the analysis of artistic movements or political developments.[42]

The political developments she lived through and wrote so passionately and intelligently about began to take such bizarre turns as the decade progressed that she felt as though she had come full circle in her writing to where she had begun: with fiction. In her old age, she wrote about this irony:

> I had in my early twenties meant to be a very superior young novelist. I actually wrote a novel, before I started writing for Ross. Virgil Thomson—who then lived in Paris finally asked me to let him read it ... [he said] I did not seem to have as much talent for fiction as for wishing to write ... In any case, European and French politics had started developing their appalling capacity for sounding like fiction, for sounding like horrifying thrillers ... For someone like me who had failed to write novels, because I lacked the creative parthenogenetical gift of being able to image fiction, as a form of self-fertilization within my own mind, I was well supplied as a journalistic reporter by what happened to millions who could not help themselves against such history ... There have been many times, in my reporting for the "Letter from Paris" for the *New Yorker* during these last seven or eight years, when it felt as if I were indeed writing fiction. This is my great recompense.[43]

ABOVE: "Anybody who loved Paris . . . is fortunate not to see it now." When Sylvia and Adrienne looked out at their beloved *arrondissement* under the Occupation, they could hardly believe their eyes.

EPILOGUE

The Occupation of Paris by the German army in June 1940 put an end to the French and expatriate community of women on the Left Bank. Those who had developed full, independent lives in Paris were reluctant to leave, yet they were forced to scatter and retreat. No longer a woman, Paris barely had any human qualities left at all. The city's soul, according to Janet Flanner, had been put up "for sale for German cash."

Perhaps it was just as well that many of the expatriates did not see their beloved city in this sad condition. Janet Flanner felt that "anybody who loved Paris and grieves at its plight is fortunate not to see it now because Paris would seem hateful."[1] Some fled to parts of the country not yet occupied; others swiftly escaped from France altogether. Late one afternoon in June 1940, Gisèle Freund was warned by friends to leave Paris immediately, and by morning she had become a refugee for the second time. Taking only her bicycle, she boarded a train for the south of France, where she expected to stay only a few months. She later departed for Argentina, and wasn't to return to France until after the liberation. Adrienne noted the timetable in her "Occupation Journal," hiding her emotions behind stony silence: "Morning at 7:40 departure Gisèle Gare d'Austerlitz. Rose at 5:00, alert at 5:10. Came

LEFT: The war took its physical toll on Noel Murphy (left), and Janet Flanner was shocked when she first saw her again after the liberation.

back from station on foot, passing in front of Saint-Geneviève."[2]

Of the French women, most stayed and managed to eke out an existence. Colette wrote "To Those Who Stay in Paris" for *Paris-Soir,* and explained that "every time there is a war, I spend it in Paris. First you have to stock up on coal, and don't forget the potatoes … You need a lot of wool sweaters to wear in the cellar during alerts."[3] Her friend Adrienne Monnier, having no other source of income, kept her shop open throughout the war. Despite pressure from family, friends, and the American government, Sylvia Beach would not consider leaving her behind. A few days before the Germans entered Paris, she wrote to Bryher,

> … A certain number of persons have gone away to what they hope will be bomb-proof country. My friend in Jersey wants me to spend the rest of the war with her there. My father suggests returning to the U.S.A.… But as far as I can see, I belong here and would only be gloomy elsewhere … [Adrienne] is now wrestling with the new No. of the Gazette which is to appear any minute … and I'm sure readers will be joyful to have it to read war or no war, and I think they will be quite reassured by the continuation of such things in the midst of trouble.

The continuation of such things did not include Sylvia's bookshop, which she had suddenly closed down after being threatened by a German officer. She managed to endure daily life in occupied Paris until August 1942, when a German truck showed up to collect her and carry her off to an internment camp in eastern France. There she remained for over six months with other American and British women who defied their governments' requests to leave the country.

ABOVE: War correspondents Janet Flanner and Ernest Hemingway, at their regular table in the Café des Deux Magots.

Although they shared a loyalty to Paris and a deep sadness about its condition, the female Modernists were divided in their response to the war. Some were committed anti-fascists and worked in the Resistance; some saw fascism and communism as equally patriarchal and authoritarian; and a few even sympathized with the fascist cause. Colette claimed that she took her "humble place among those who did nothing except wait."[4] Actually she appealed to anyone who would listen, including numerous Nazis and their French collaborators, as she sought to find, and then secure the release of, her Jewish husband, Maurice Goudeker, who was arrested in 1941. Gertrude Stein, who had served as an ambulance driver in France during the First World War, wrote to Janet Flanner, "neither we nor Noel [Murphy] are going to go to war. England and France could do as they wished."

As the Germans invaded France, Janet Flanner and Solita Solano left

189

Noel Murphy on her farm in Orgeval and set sail for New York. Noel survived from her garden vegetables and a false identity card which gave her an Irish name but French nationality. It is possible she was a Nazi collaborator, as some people accused her of being, although Janet herself refused to believe it. Noel also spent five months in the same detention center as Sylvia Beach.

Hemingway showed up with a BBC crew to "liberate" his favorite street, rue de l'Odéon, right after Germany surrendered Paris. He had the nerve to ask Adrienne Monnier, who loved good food, how she managed to survive without some sort of collaboration with the Nazis. By way of reply, she hinted that there are many ways of carrying out sabotage.

Janet Flanner, Bryher, and Nancy Cunard were also anti-fascist and, not being French, could afford to be more vocal about it than Adrienne Monnier. Nancy Cunard had initially retreated to Santiago and Mexico City at the outbreak of war, but when France fell to the Germans, she headed back to Europe (something easier said than done at that time) to do what she could. She considered it "my war too—insofar as it is (if only partly) against Fascism."[5] From London she worked with Free French organizations, translated a book on the French Resistance, and compiled an anthology of poetry, *Poems for France,* which was published in 1944.

Bryher, as already noted, contributed not only her family wealth but also her own efforts to the Resistance by helping German Jews and radicals escape through Switzerland.

She felt she did no more than any human being who believed in morality would do, by saving over a hundred lives before having to flee herself. Of all the people she helped, only two did not make it to safety; one of these was the writer and philosopher Walter Benjamin, who was stopped at the Spanish border and took his own life. In 1940, Bryher escaped at zero hour across the Swiss border and back to London, in the midst of the Blitz. There she lived out the rest of the war with H.D. and their daughter Perdita.

Janet Flanner knew it was time to leave when her "Letter from Paris" was censored in October 1939. Shari Benstock describes her departure from Paris as marking the end of the era:

ABOVE: Sylvia celebrated the liberation of Paris by flying an American flag outside her window, and by writing a letter to Bryher "after five years of silence."

Janet Flanner was one of the last to leave, and when she fled Paris on the afternoon of 4 October 1939, she ran from encroaching darkness augured by the sounds of military aircraft and marching armies. The door of the culture she helped to create on the Paris Left Bank closed behind her.[6]

New York, London, Territet in Switzerland; Fiesole in Italy; Bilignin in France; Santiago, Buenos Aires, Mexico City—from these as well as other settings, their friendships persisted across the distances. Rarely

LEFT: *Life* magazine reported on the reunion of Americans Sylvia Beach, Janet Flanner, and Ernest Hemingway upon the liberation of Paris.

could correspondence get through, and when it did, as with Natalie Barney's letters to Gertrude and Alice, the censorship prevented much from being said or read. More often friends relied on word of mouth, and in the absence of any news, blind faith. Bryher afterwards wrote

> of the joy H.D. and I had felt when a letter from [Sylvia Beach] had reached us in London after five years of silence, it seemed impossible that it could fall on the floor with a newspaper, a bill and some unimportant trifles, with your own handwriting on the envelope.[7]

It seems equally impossible that Janet Flanner, as a war correspondent, found time to read Gertrude Stein's *Paris France,* yet it was important enough to her that she managed to write some encouraging words to Gertrude about it, and review it in *The New Yorker.*

> Dear Gertrude,
>
> It's a *fine* book, full of just that sort of sense you have for things other people make nonsense out of—I enjoyed reading it very much … and have found it very fertilizing, it gives me new notions about many things …

Gertrude and Alice escaped to their summer house in Bilignin, American Jews defying the Nazi occupiers despite pleas from the American embassy to flee from France altogether. They received a letter there from Janet Flanner, instructing them that

> both of you must stay there with rocks and fresh eggs and air and Basket as long as possible—Love to you both, indeed all three [though I know Basket only slightly—] And my very sincere thanks—Yours Faithfully Janet

If Janet felt that Gertrude and Alice and their new poodle (named Basket as the first had been) were in idyllic retreat from the war, Gertrude and Alice themselves felt they were living through the war's darkest days, and that it was Janet who was in retreat. Upon receiving Janet's book review, Gertrude wrote to her in New York:

> Some one just sent me your review of Paris France and it is a beautiful review and has pleased me enormously, and thanks and thanks again, you know Janet even in the darkest days we talked about you, I used to say and it was only three days ago that I was saying it again, I am so sorry Janet was not in France for it all, she would have liked being here and Alice always answered, perhaps she would not have liked it at all and then we argued, well Janet, what is the answer. Oh Janet, someday well not too far away, you and Noel will come and spend that promised week and we could tell you so much. When are you coming back, well until you do come back Alice and I will continue to argue whether you would have liked being here or whether you would not have liked being here, bless you, come back to us soon and thanks and thanks again for the perfect review, lots of love from us both, always Gtde.

"Come back to us soon" is the refrain of the many letters written between friends divided by war. Returning from Italy, where she and Romaine Brooks sympathized with Mussolini, held anti-Semitic views, and sunbathed in trenches to avoid being spotted by aircraft, Natalie Barney wrote to Gertrude and Alice in Bilignin:

> Dear Gertrude and Alice dear, ... I have dreamed of getting

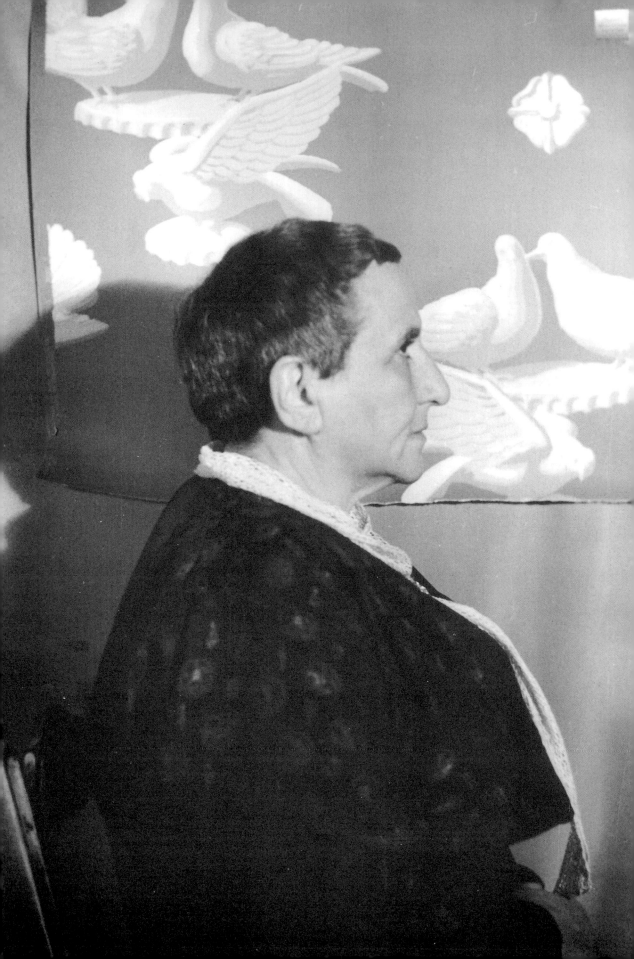

back to our old quarter so long, that, like a somnambulist, I shall find my way to your door, and see the doves of your bedroom flutter, and the easy chairs contain us as before, and your portrait seating you above us, looks down; uniting past and present to whatever future we have yet to live through —may it be in Paris ...

Love, Natalie and my friend Romaine

Gertrude did not have much future left, although she did live it through in Paris. She died of cancer in 1946, a year after the war ended. Devastated, Alice wrote, "I wish to God we had gone together as I always so fatuously thought we would—a bomb—a shipwreck—just anything but this."[8]

Natalie's condolences acknowledged the importance of Alice's work to Gertrude's career:

Ah Alice what can I send you now? No words can match such a loss ... Perhaps her works, which you will continue later on, may bring a feeling of accomplishing those duties which you have always filled to the utmost ... I can never separate you from Gertrude nor Gertrude from you. So let her remain there ever between us uniting us more closely than ever ...

The close network of friends kept each other informed of Alice's daily trials and tribulations in "staying on alone." Sylvia reported to Bryher about such mundane difficulties as what to do about the animals:

[July 9th, 1947] Alice Toklas came to see me one day. She said she was so glad to hear Bryher was coming to Paris ... Basket pulls too hard when she takes him for walks. He had a fit of jealousy when she took in a cat, and got eczema, the vet said entirely on account of the cat. He refused to come into the salon any more until Alice got rid of the cat ... With much love dear Bryher ... Please give my love to H.D.

LEFT: Natalie Barney longed to get back to Paris and see the doves of Gertrude's bedroom flutter, but they were actually pigeons on the grass, alas.

ABOVE: Janet wrote on the back of this photo: "The most widowed woman I know. I said this to Alice the first time I saw her after Gertrude's death."

On many days, however, Alice had more substantial causes for despair. When Picasso's painting of Gertrude was collected for the Metropolitan Museum in New York, and Picasso came by to say farewell to it, "It was another parting and completely undid me."[9]

What became of the rest of Gertrude and Alice's art collection is a sad, often repeated story. Since Gertrude and Alice had of course no legal connection, Gertrude's nephew's children contested Alice's right to the collection, bought for virtually nothing but by now valued at over six million dollars. Without the paintings, one or two of which she could decide to part with *in extremis,* Alice did not have enough cash for her daily expenses. Janet called upon mutual old friends and created and administered a fund for Alice's support. She wrote to a friend, "It drives me mad that Alice is driven to the generous charity of her friends when she is in reality an HEIRESS—" Publicly she wrote about the fate of these famous paintings, perhaps in the hope that other contributors would come forward. But when Margaret Anderson mentioned to Janet that "you gave so many interesting details about Gertrude's will that I suppose you were swamped with appreciative letters," Janet replied, "Not at all, not one. No one seemed to care."

Readers of *The New Yorker* may not have cared, but Alice's friends certainly did. Thorton Wilder, Bryher, and Janet Flanner herself were among those who supported Alice in her old age, after she could no longer afford to write such proud letters as she had in 1956: "So, dear Bryher, I am returning your check but keeping as a lovely gift your thought in sending it."

Gertrude's was the first in a long string of deaths, stretched across four decades, which interrupted these extraordinary friendships. Adrienne Monnier was the next to go; plagued by maddening, unrelenting sounds in her ears, she took her own life in 1955. Although Sylvia was glad that Adrienne had finally found peace and quiet, she wrote to Bryher, "it is very hard for me who have lost Adrienne who was everything in my life …" Like Alice's hopes for a bomb or a shipwreck that would have taken them both, Sylvia too "would have liked so much to have left at the same time as Adrienne," which Adrienne had proposed, knowing how hard it would be for Sylvia without her. The rue de l'Odéon which had been her home for so many decades "might be anywhere else with Adrienne gone—everything gone. Surgical

ABOVE: Old friends Sylvia Beach (right) and Bryher in 1959, at an exhibit on Paris in the twenties, based on Sylvia's personal possessions.

darling, should have sent the photographs
earlier, but anything to do with us bothers
me, the pain is so unequal that i just natually
avoid it when possible, its been so long a time
too its too much. i have kept the pictures i
love and that belong to me alone.

i have a trembly right hand so the typing,
no hangover havent had a drink about ten years —
spring is here but as rachel carson said it is
silent, the people have taken everything.

i love you as always.

Thelma

LEFT: Thelma and Djuna:
still tortured forty years
later.

instruments in Shakespeare & Company now and preferably at the
Amis des Livres as well."

Bryher responded with messages of comfort and love, but found
herself next on the receiving end of the condolences. H.D. had a
stroke and passed away three months later. Alice wrote to Bryher
soon after:

> The other evening I hobbled to a lecture … and there spoke
> for a moment to Sylvia. When I asked her for news of you and
> H.D. she told me [of] H.D.'s death. It was inexpressibly sad
> for me … Nothing will replace for you the wonderful person
> she was … My deep sympathy, dear Bryher, and affectionate
> appreciation. Alice.

The one person who outlived all the rest was the isolated and embit-
tered Djuna Barnes, who marked each death as "one more nail in
our own coffins."[10] Back in New York, she saw no one, not even
her beloved Thelma Wood, although they spoke occasionally on the

phone. In 1964, Djuna wrote of Thelma, "Still beautiful? I hear not, how can one be at 62. I think she has gained weight, wears glasses, and has white in her hair; poor child, she never knew such things could happen to her."[11] Thelma developed cancer of the spine and spent her final years bedridden. Berenice Abbott had stayed in touch with Thelma throughout the decades and visited her just before her death that, Berenice reported, she met bravely and philosophically.

Djuna Barnes admitted that they were in "the winter of our world" but she was not one to fall back on nostalgia. If she expressed any regrets, they were not sentimental ones. She wrote to Solita Solano in 1951, "Sometimes I think I have made a mistake in this matter of 'all for art' and nothing whatsoever for money." When *The Little Review* was reprinted as a book in the late sixties, Djuna was not concerned with drawing public attention to the "lost masterpieces" of the era or even with seeing something of hers back in print long after she had been forgotten. She wrote to Solita about potential royalties:

> I see that the *Little Review* has been reprinted by some crook (that's what they are) in toto, and gather that no author has seen so much as the thin side of a dime for their part in it? Will you ask Margaret about this?
> … This is one of these upstart publishers tricks.

Djuna Barnes was not the only one to remain true to form as she grew older. At the age of 90, Natalie Barney still persisted with her lifelong cause, that of bringing recognition to the work of the many women artists and writers who were her friends. She wrote to Janet Flanner in 1967 as though it were still 1927, asking if she would write something in *The New Yorker* about the paintings of Romaine Brooks.

But if Natalie's role hadn't changed, Janet's certainly had: just as she had reported on and publicized the activities of her dear friends in the prewar years, now with the passing decades she became the chronicler of their deaths. One by one, she paid posthumous respects to each in the pages of *The New Yorker,* rarely revealing how much her own life must have been diminished by each loss.

Her public letters are staggering evidence of the contributions this extraordinary group of women, singly and together, made to western culture. But it is the private letters, both sent and received, that document the vital, tenacious web of friendships, spun long ago in Paris. These friendships, sparked by something so intangible as the promise of Paris at a particular moment in history, made it possible for them to create the cultural legacy they have left for us. Fifteen years after Gertrude's death, Alice sent Janet Flanner and Solita Solano a postcard: "My dearest dears … Paris and the French still seduce me … Love love love Alice."

Notes

PREFACE TO THE 2013 EDITION

1. Thanks to Sebastian Claesson, a journalist in Malmö, Sweden for bringing Nadine Hwong to my attention.
2. An excellent defense which addresses the charges point by point with deep historical insight and nuance is Renate Stendhal's "Why the Witch-hunt Against Gertrude Stein," *Tikkun Magazine*, June 4, 2012.
3. Charles Bernstein, "Gertrude Stein's War Years: Setting the Record Straight," https://jacket2.org/feature/gertrude-steins-war-years-setting-record-straight, May 9, 2012.

INTRODUCTION: PARIS WAS A WOMAN

1. Frederic Lefèvre, quoted in the *Paris Tribune* (8 June 1924), reprinted in Hugh Ford, ed., *The Left Bank Revisited: Selections from the Paris Tribune 1917–1934* (University Park: Penn State University Press, 1972), p. 96.
2. Bryher, *The Heart to Artemis* (London: Collins, 1963), p. 226.
3. Andrew Field, *Djuna: The Life and Times of Djuna Barnes* (New York: Putnam, 1983), pp. 133–134.
4. Gertrude Stein, *Everybody's Autobiography* (New York: Vintage Press, 1973), pp. 102–103.
5. Katherine Anne Porter, "Gertrude Stein: A Self-Portrait," *Harper's Magazine* 195 (December 1947): p. 522.
6. Jessie Fauset, *Paris Tribune* (1 February 1923), reprinted in Hugh Ford, ed., *The Left Bank Revisited*, op. cit., pp. 47–48.
7. From a letter written by Gertrude Stein in 1939 to Gotham Book Mart's owner Miss Steloff in New York, who published it in her bookstore catalogue.

CHAPTER 1: ODÉONIA: THE COUNTRY OF BOOKS

1. Adrienne Monnier, "Souvenirs de l'autre guerre," *The Very Rich Hours of Adrienne Monnier: An Intimate Portrait of the Literary and Artistic Life in Paris Between the Wars*, translated, with an introduction and commentaries, by Richard McDougall (New York: Charles Scribner's Sons, 1976), p.11.
2. Janet Flanner, "The Infinite Pleasure: Sylvia Beach," *Janet Flanner's World: Uncollected Writings 1932–1975* (New York and London: Harcourt Brace Jovanovich, 1979), p. 310.
3. Noel Riley Fitch, *Sylvia Beach and the Lost Generation: A History of Literary Paris in the Twenties and Thirties* (New York and London: W.W. Norton and Co., 1983), p. 11.
4. Sylvia Beach, *Shakespeare and Company* (New York: Harcourt, Brace and Co., 1956), p. 16.

5. Adrienne Monnier, "Memorial de la rue de l'Odéon," quoted in *The Very Rich Hours of Adrienne Monnier*, op. cit., p. 40.

6. Katherine Anne Porter to Sylvia Beach, 6 February 1956, published in *Sylvia Beach: 1887–1962* (Paris: Mercure de France, 1963), p. 154.

7. Sylvia Beach, *Shakespeare and Company*, op. cit., p. 47.

8. Sergei M. Eisenstein to Sylvia Beach, December 11,1933, published in *Sylvia Beach: 1887–1962*, op. cit., p. 125.

9. Sylvia Beach to Bryher, 13 January 1936, in the Bryher collection of the Beinecke Rare Book and Manuscript Library, Yale University.

10. Quoted in Noel Riley Fitch, *Sylvia Beach and the Lost Generation,* op. cit., p. 25.

11. Janet Flanner, "The Great Amateur Publisher," *Sylvia Beach: 1887–1962* op. cit., p. 48.

12. Sylvia Beach, *Shakespeare and Company*, op. cit., p. 27.

13. Bryher, "For Sylvia," *Sylvia Beach: 1887–1962,* op. cit., p. 18.

14. Bryher, *The Heart to Artemis* (London: Collins, 1963), p. 211.

15. Sylvia Beach, "A Letter to Bryher" written for Bryher's birthday in 1950. Bryher collection, Beinecke Rare Book and Manuscript Library, Yale University.

16. Jules Romains, quoted in Adrienne Monnier, *The Very Rich Hours of Adrienne Monnier,* op. cit., p. 14.

17. Interview with Gisèle Freund, June 1992, for the *Paris Was a Woman* film project.

18. Adrienne Monnier, "In the Country of Faces," *The Very Rich Hours of Adrienne Monnier,* op. cit., pp. 231–232.

19. Simone de Beauvoir, preface to Gisèle Freund, *James Joyce in Paris,* quoted in Adrienne Monnier, *The Very Rich Hours of Adrienne Monnier,* ibid., p. 491.

20. Sylvia Beach to Bryher, September 21,1935, in the Bryher collection, Beinecke Rare Book and Manuscript Library, Yale University.

21. Sylvia Beach, Shakespeare and Company, op. cit., p. 29.

22. Bryher, *The Heart to Artemis*, op. cit., p. 211.

23. Sylvia Beach, quoted in Jackson Matthews, "My Sylvia Beach," *Sylvia Beach 1887–1962,* op. cit., p. 25.

24. Janet Flanner, "The Infinite Pleasure: Sylvia Beach," *Janet Flanner's World: Uncollected Writings 1932–1975,* op. cit., p. 309.

25. Jackson Matthews, "My Sylvia Beach," *Sylvia Beach: 1887–1962*, op. cit., p. 26.

26. Sylvia Beach, *Shakespeare and Company*, op. cit., pp. 58 and 88.

27. Janet Flanner, "The Great Amateur Publisher," *Sylvia Beach: 1887–1962,* op. cit., pp. 46–51.

28. James Joyce, quoted in Noel Riley Fitch, *Sylvia Beach and the Lost Generation,* op. cit., p. 328.

29. Sylvia Beach, *Shakespeare and Company*, op. cit., pp. 58–60.

30. Interview with Sam Steward, July 1992, for the *Paris Was a Woman* film project.

31. Interview with Gisèle Freund, June 1992, for the *Paris Was a Woman* film project.

32. Sylvia Beach to Holly Beach, quoted in Noel Riley Fitch, *Sylvia Beach and the Lost Generation,* op. cit., p. 318.

33. Robert McAlmon to Gertrude Stein, in the Stein collection, Beinecke Rare Book and Manuscript Library, Yale University.

34. T.S. Eliot, "Miss Sylvia Beach," *Sylvia Beach: 1887–1962*, op. cit., p. 9.

35. Interview with Gisèle Freund, June 1992, for the *Paris Was a Woman* film project.
36. Jean Amrouche, quoted in Adrienne Monnier, *The Very Rich Hours of Adrienne Monnier,* op. cit., pp. 60–61.
37. Shari Benstock, *Women of the Left Bank* (Austin: University of Texas Press, 1986 and London: Virago Press, 1987), p. 228.
38. Bryher, *The Heart to Artemis*, op. cit., p. 213.
39. Janet Flanner, "The Infinite Pleasure," *Janet Flanner's World*, op. cit., p. 314.
40. Sylvia Beach, *Shakespeare and Company*, op. cit., p. 215.

CHAPTER 2: THE WRITER AND HER MUSE

All quotes from letters not listed below are to be found in the Gertrude Stein collection, Beinecke Rare Book and Manuscript Library of Yale University.

1. Alice B. Toklas, *What is Remembered* (New York: Holt, Rinehart and Winston, 1963), p. 23. Also, Alice B. Toklas, interviewed by Roland E. Duncan, Paris, November 1952. Audiotape in the Bancroft Library, University of California at Berkeley.
2. Katherine Anne Porter, "Gertrude Stein: A Self-Portrait," *Harper's Magazine* 195 (December 1947): p. 519.
3. Janet Flanner, "Introduction: Frame For Some Portraits," *Two: Gertrude Stein and Her Brother and Other Early Portraits [1908–1912]: Volume One of the Yale Edition of the Unpublished Writings of Gertrude Stein* (New Haven: Yale University Press, 1951), p. x.
4. Catharine R. Stimpson, "Gertrice/Altrude: Stein, Toklas, and the Paradox of the Happy Marriage," *Mothering the Mind: Twelve Studies of Writers and Their Silent Partners,* eds. Ruth Perry and Martine Watson Brownley (New York and London: Holmes and Meir, 1984), p. 126.
5. Natalie Clifford Barney, "Foreword," *As Fine as Melanctha: Volume Four of the Yale Edition of the Unpublished Writings of Gertrude Stein* (New Haven: Yale University Press, 1954).
6. Gertrude Stein, *Everybody's Autobiography* (New York: Vintage Press, 1973), p.87.
7. Catharine R. Stimpson, "Gertrice/Altrude: Stein, Toklas, and the Paradox of the Happy Marriage," op. cit., p. 133.
8. Judy Grahn, *Really Reading Gertrude Stein* (Freedom: The Crossing Press, 1989), pp. 6–7.
9. Natalie Clifford Barney, "Foreword," *As Fine As Melanctha,* op. cit.
10. Bryher, *The Heart to Artemis* (London: Collins, 1963), p. 215.
11. William Carlos Williams, "MANIFESTO: in the form of a criticism of the works of Gertrude Stein," manuscript in the Stein collection, Beinecke Rare Book and Manuscript Library, Yale University.
12. Bryher, *The Heart to Artemis,* op. cit., p. 208.
13. Pavel Tchelitchew, Martin A. Ryerson Lecture on Gertrude Stein, 20 February 1961 at the Yale Gallery of Fine Arts. This quote is from the transcript of the audiotape, Stein collection, Beinecke Rare Book and Manuscript Library, Yale University.

14. Janet Flanner, "Foreword: Frame For Some Portraits," op. cit., p. xvi.

15. Alice B. Toklas, *What is Remembered,* op. cit., p. 136.

16. Janet Flanner, *An American in Paris: Profile of an Interlude between Two Wars* (London: Hamish Hamilton, 1940), pp. 83–84.

17. Pavel Tchelitchew, Martin A. Ryerson Lecture, op. cit.

18. Undated letter from Gertrude Stein to a Miss Clair who had asked for biographical information in preparation for the publication of *Tender Buttons.*

19. Janet Flanner, "Introduction: Frame For Some Portraits," op. cit., p. xi.

20. Janet Flanner, "Paris in the Twenties," CBS Television, broadcast date 17 April 1960.

21. Sylvia Beach, *Shakespeare and Company* (New York: Harcourt, Brace and Co., 1956), p. 31.

22. Natalie Clifford Barney, "Foreword," *As Fine as Melanctha,* op. cit. Reprinted in Linda Simon, ed., *Gertrude Stein Remembered* (Lincoln: University of Nebraska Press, 1994), p. 30.

23. Pavel Tchelitchew, Martin A. Ryerson Lecture, op. cit.

24. Interview with Samuel Steward, July 1992, for the *Paris Was a Woman* film project.

25. Samuel Putnam, *Paris Was Our Mistress* (New York: Viking Press, 1947), p. 136.

26. John Richardson, "Picasso and Gertrude Stein: Mano a Mano, Tête-a-Tête," *The New York Times* (10 February 1991): p. 36.

27. Pavel Tchelitchew, Martin A. Ryerson Lecture, op. cit.

28. Gertrude Stein, interviewed at Columbia University on NBC Radio, November 12, 1934.

29. Alice B. Toklas, interviewed by Roland E. Duncan, Paris, November 1952.

30. Richard Wright, "Gertrude Stein's story is drenched in Hitler's horrors," *PM Magazine* (11 March 1945).

31. Jacqueline Morreau, "Introduction" to Gertrude Stein, *Wars I Have Seen* (London: Brilliance Books, 1984), p. xiv.

32. Alice B. Toklas, interviewed by Roland E. Duncan, Paris, November 1952.

33. Virgil Thomson, "A Portrait of Gertrude Stein," *A Virgil Thomson Reader* (Boston: Houghton Mifflin Co., 1981), p. 75.

34. Katherine Anne Porter, "Gertrude Stein: A Self-Portrait," op. cit., p. 527.

35. Janet Flanner, "Paris in the Twenties," CBS Television, broadcast 17 April 1960.

36. Gertrude Stein, *Everybody's Autobiography,* op. cit., p.47.

37. Janet Flanner, "Introduction: Frame For Some Portraits," op. cit., p. xii.

38. Gertrude Stein, in Peter Neagoe, ed., *Americans Abroad* (The Hague: The Servire Press, 1932), p. 418.

39. Alice B. Toklas, interviewed by Roland E. Duncan, Paris, November 1952.

CHAPTER 3: AMAZONES ET SIRÈNES

All quotes by Natalie Barney not identified below are from her unpublished autobiography, *Memoirs of a European American,* in the Fonds Littéraire Jacques Doucet. All letters to her not identified below are housed in the Doucet collection; all other unidentified letters in this chapter can be found in the Stein collection, Beinecke Rare Book and Manuscript Library, Yale University.

1. George Wickes, *The Amazon of Letters* (New York: G.P. Putnam's Sons, 1976), p. 7.
2. André Germain, *Les Clés de Proust* (Paris: Sun [1953]), cited in Wickes, ibid., p. 93.
3. Natalie Barney, quoted in Wickes, ibid., p. 44.
4. Natalie Barney, quoted in Wickes, ibid., p. 48.
5. Marguerite Yourcenar, quoted in Jean Chalon, *Portrait of a Seductress: The World of Natalie Barney,* trans. Carol Barko (New York: Crown Publishers, 1979), p. 221.
6. Solita Solano, "The Hotel Napoléon Bonaparte," in John C. Broderick, "Paris between the Wars: An Unpublished Memoir by Solita Solano," *Quarterly Journal of the Library of Congress,* 34 (October 1977): pp. 309–310.
7. Truman Capote, quoted in Wickes, op. cit., p. 255.
8. Natalie Clifford Barney, in a dedication to Berthe Cleyrergue dated 1929, quoted in Chalon, p. 147.
9. Interview with Berthe Cleyrergue, July 1992, for the *Paris Was a Woman* film project.
10. Janet Flanner, interviewed in Wickes, op. cit., p. 261.
11. Janet Flanner, introduction to Colette, *The Pure and the Impure,* transl. Herma Brifault (London: Penguin Books, 1971), p. 6.
12. Janet Flanner, introduction to Colette, *The Pure and the Impure,* ibid., p. 8.
13. Herbert Lottman, *Colette: A Life* (London: Secker and Warburg, 1991), p. 27.
14. Colette, preface to *Claudine at School,* transl. Antonia White (London: Penguin, 1963), pp. 5–6.
15. Colette, *Earthly Paradise: An Autobiography Drawn from her Lifetime Writings* by Robert Phelps (New York: Farrar, Straus & Giroux, 1966).
16. Janet Flanner, introduction to Colette, *The Pure and the Impure,* op. cit., p. 9.
17. Janet Flanner, in a draft of a speech in tribute to Colette, July 1966, in the Flanner/Solano papers, Library of Congress.
18. Letter from Colette to Janet Flanner, n.d., Flanner/Solano papers, Library of Congress.
19. Truman Capote, quoted in Wickes, op. cit., p. 256.
20. Interview with Berthe Cleyrergue, July 1992, for the *Paris Was a Woman* film project.
21. Natalie Clifford Barney, "Foreword," *As Fine as Melanctha,* op. cit. Reprinted in Linda Simon, ed., *Gertrude Stein Remembered* (Lincoln: University of Nebraska Press, 1994), pp. 31–32.
22. Natalie Clifford Barney, "Foreword," *As Fine as Melanctha,* ibid., pp. 31–32.
23. Virgil Thomson, quoted in Wickes, op. cit., p. 248.
24. Elizabeth Eyre de Lanux, quoted in Wickes, ibid., p. 242.
25. Gabriel-Louis Pringue, *Trente Ans de Diners en Ville,* quoted in Chalon, op. cit., p. 160.
26. Janet Flanner, quoted in Wickes, op. cit., p. 261.
27. Letter from Dolly Wilde to Janet Flanner, n.d., Flanner/Solano papers, Library of Congress.
28. Janet Flanner, quoted in Wickes, op. cit., p. 260.
29. Interview with Gisèle Freund, July 1992, for the *Paris Was a Woman* film project.

30. Sylvia Beach to Bryher, 15 January 1953, Bryher collection of the Beinecke Rare Book and Manuscript Library, Yale University.

31. Sylvia Beach, *Shakespeare and Company* (New York: Harcourt, Brace and Co., 1956), p. 115.

32. *Colette: Catalogue de l'exposition* (Paris: Bibliotheque Nationale: 1973), pp. 163–164, quoted in Lotman, op. cit., p. 207.

33. Janet Flanner, *Paris Was Yesterday: 1925–1939* (New York: Harcourt Brace Jovanovich, 1988), p. 48.

34. Natalie Clifford Barney, "Foreword," *As Fine as Melanctha,* op. cit. Reprinted in Linda Simon, ed., *Gertrude Stein Remembered,* op. cit., pp. 33–34.

35. Gertrude Stein, *Picasso* (Boston: Beacon Press, 1959), p. 8.

36. Germaine Beaumont to Solita Solano, 1964, in the Flanner/Solano papers, Library of Congress.

CHAPTER 4: CITY OF DARK NIGHTS

All letters to Djuna Barnes are to be found in the McKeldin Library, University of Maryland at College Park. All letters from Djuna Barnes to Emily Holmes Coleman are from the Emily Holmes Coleman papers at the University of Delaware Library. All letters to Natalie Barney are from the Fonds Littéraire Jacques Doucet. All other letters where no source is indicated are from the Beinecke Rare Book Room and Manuscript Library, Yale University.

1. Natalie Barney, quoted in George Wickes, *The Amazon of Letters* (New York: G.P. Putnam's Sons, 1976), p. 180.

2. Kathryn Hulme, *Undiscovered Country* (Boston: Atlantic-Little, Brown, 1966), pp. 37–39.

3. Eugene Jolas, *Paris Tribune* (20 July 1924), reprinted in Hugh Ford, ed., *The Left Bank Revisited* (University Park: Penn State University Press, 1972), p. 97.

4. Virgil Thomson, "A Portrait of Gertrude Stein," *A Virgil Thomson Reader* (Boston: Houghton Mifflin Co., 1981), p. 69.

5. Janet Flanner, "Introduction," *Paris Was Yesterday: 1925–1939* (New York: Harcourt Brace Jovanovich, 1988), pp. xvii–xviii.

6. Janet Flanner, "The Infinite Pleasure: Sylvia Beach," *Janet Flanner's World: Uncollected Writings 1932–1975* (New York and London: Harcourt Brace Jovanovich, 1979), p. 309.

7. Djuna Barnes, I *Could Never Be Lonely Without a Husband: Interviews by Djuna Barnes,* ed. Alyce Barry (London: Virago Press, 1987), p. 288.

8. Sylvia Beach, *Shakespeare and Company* (New York: Harcourt, Brace and Co., 1956), p. 112.

9. Andrew Field, *Djuna: The Life and Times of Djuna Barnes* (New York: Putnam's, 1983), p. 84.

10. Allan Ross MacDougall, ed., *Letters of Edna St. Vincent Millay* (New York: Harper and Brothers, 1952), p. 116.

11. Interview with Berthe Cleyrergue, June 1992, for the *Paris Was a Woman* film project.

12. See Cheryl Plumb, "Revising Nightwood: 'a kind of glee of despair,'" *The Review of Contemporary Fiction* 13, no.3 (Fall 1993): p. 158.

13. Andrew Field, *Djuna: The Life and Times of Djuna Barnes*, op. cit., p. 147.

14. Djuna Barnes, *The Paris Tribune* (2 September 1931), reprinted in Hugh Ford, ed., *The Left Bank Revisited*, op. cit., p. 142.

15. Sylvia Beach, *Shakespeare and Company*, op. cit., p. 112.

16. Shari Benstock, *Women of the Left Bank* (Austin: University of Texas Press, 1986 and London: Virago Press, 1987), p. 245.

17. Djuna Barnes to Solita Solano, 22 May 1964, Flanner/Solano papers, Library of Congress.

CHAPTER 5: LETTERS FROM PARIS

All letters to Janet Flanner or Solita Solano and all unpublished writings by Janet Flanner not identified below can be found in the Flanner/Solano papers of the Library of Congress. All other unidentified writings by Janet Flanner are from her "Letter from Paris" column in *The New Yorker*.

1. Quoted in Brenda Wineapple, *Genêt: A Biography of Janet Flanner* (New York: Ticknor & Fields, 1989), p. 55.

2. G.Y. Dryanski, "Genêt Recalls Paris in the 20's," *Washington Post* (1967). Newspaper clipping from the Flanner/Solano papers in the Library of Congress.

3. Quoted in Brenda Wineapple, op. cit., p. 21.

4. Solita Solano, "The Hotel Napoléon Bonaparte," in John C. Broderick, "Paris between the Wars: An Unpublished Memoir by Solita Solano," *Quarterly Journal of the Library of Congress* 34 (October 1977): p. 313. According to John C. Broderick's footnotes, Janet interpolated the phrase "of an intense blue" into Solita's manuscript.

5. Solita Solano, "The Hotel Napoléon Bonaparte," ibid., in John C. Broderick, pp. 308–309.

6. Solita Solano, "The Hotel Napoléon Bonaparte," ibid., in John C. Broderick, pp. 312–313.

7. Jane Cole Grant, *Ross, The New Yorker and Me* (New York: Reynal & Co, 1968), p. 223.

8. Eugene Jolas, *Paris Tribune* (28 December 1924), reprinted in Hugh Ford, ed., *The Left Bank Revisited: Selections from the Paris Tribune 1917–1934* (University Park: Penn State University Press, 1972), p. 261.

9. Solita Solano, quoted in John C. Broderick, op. cit., p. 306.

10. Janet Flanner, draft of speech to The American Institute of Arts and Letters, in the Flanner/Solano papers, Library of Congress, n.d.

11. Patrick O'Higgins, "In Her Own Words: Janet (Genêt) Flanner on her 'Pets' from 50 Years in Paris (De Gaulle Wasn't One of Them)," *People* 3, no.7 (24 February 1975): p. 62.

12. Patrick O'Higgins, "In Her Own Words," *People*, ibid., pp. 60–61.

13. Janet Flanner, "Introduction," *Paris Was Yesterday: 1925–1939* (New York: Harcourt Brace Jovanovich, 1988), p. xix.

14. Jane Cole Grant, *Ross, The New Yorker and Me*, op. cit., pp. 223–4.

15. Janet Flanner, draft of speech on Colette, July 1966, Flanner/Solano papers of the Library of Congress.

16. Janet Flanner, Introduction, *City of Love,* ed. Daniel Talbot (New York: Dell, 1955).

17. Berenice Abbott, quoted in Morrill Cody, *The Women of Montparnasse* (Cranbury, NJ: Cornwall Books, 1984), p. 163.

18. *Paris Tribune* (20 May 1927), reprinted in Hugh Ford, ed., *The Left Bank Revisited,* op. cit., pp. 83–84.

19. Bryher, *The Heart to Artemis* (London: Collins, 1963), p. 208.

20. Janet Flanner, "A Life on a Cloud: Margaret Anderson," *Janet Flanner's World: Uncollected Writings 1932–1975* (New York and London: Harcourt Brace Jovanovich, 1979), p. 320.

21. Margaret Anderson, quoted in Morrill Cody, *The Women of Montparnasse,* op. cit., p. 151.

22. Margaret Anderson, "Introduction," *The Little Review Anthology* (New York: Hermitage House, 1953).

23. Ezra Pound to Margaret Anderson, n.d. [January 1917] quoted in Gillian Hanscombe and Virginia L. Smyers, *Writing for their Lives: The Modernist Women 1910–1914* (Boston: Northeastern University Press, 1988 and London: The Women's Press, 1987), p. 181.

24. Robert Sage, *Paris Tribune* (18 January 1931), reprinted in Hugh Ford, ed., *The Left Bank Revisited,* op. cit., p. 71.

25. H.D. to Amy Lowell (19 September 1917), quoted in Gillian Hanscombe and Virginia L. Smyers, *Writing for their Lives,* op. cit., p. 183.

26. Margaret Anderson, *My Thirty Years' War* (New York: Covici Friede, 1930), quoted in Janet Flanner, "A Life on a Cloud: Margaret Anderson," op. cit., pp. 323–324.

27. Janet Flanner, "A Life On a Cloud: Margaret Anderson," ibid., p. 326.

28. Margaret Anderson, quoted in Janet Flanner, "A Life On a Cloud: Margaret Anderson," ibid., p. 326.

29. Janet Flanner, "A Life On a Cloud: Margaret Anderson," ibid., p. 326.

30. Margaret Anderson, *My Thirty Years' War,* op. cit., p. 102; Shari Benstock, *Women of the Left Bank* (Austin: University of Texas Press, 1986 and London: Virago Press, 1987), p. 379.

31. T.S. Eliot to Gertrude Stein, 21 April 1925, Stein collection, Beinecke Rare Book and Manuscript Library, Yale University.

32. Janet Flanner, "A Life On a Cloud: Margaret Anderson," op. cit., p. 325.

33. Eugene Jolas, *Paris Tribune* (28 December 1924), reprinted in Hugh Ford, ed. *The Left Bank Revisited,* op. cit., p. 261.

34. Bryher, *The Heart to Artemis,* op. cit., p. 208.

35. H.D. to Ezra Pound, n.d. [1929], quoted in Janice S. Robinson, *H.D.: The Life and Work of an American Poet* (Boston: Houghton Mifflin Co., 1982), p. 266.

36. *Paris Tribune* (26 January 1930) reprinted in Hugh Ford, ed., *The Left Bank Revisited,* op. cit., p. 252–3.

37. Solita Solano, "Nancy Cunard: Brave Poet, Indomitable Rebel," in Hugh Ford, ed., *Nancy Cunard: Brave Poet, Indomitable Rebel* (Philadelphia: Chilton Book Co., 1968). p. 76.

38. Andrew Field, *Djuna: The Life and Times of Djuna Barnes* (New York: Putnam's, 1983), p. 104.

39. Brenda Wineapple, *Genêt: A Biography of Janet Flanner,* op. cit., p. 93.

40. Solita Solano, "Both Banks of the Seine," *D.A.C. News* (20 February 1932): p. 50.

41. Jane Cole Grant, *The New Yorker, Ross, and Me,* op. cit., p. 224.

42. Shari Benstock, *Women of the Left Bank,* op. cit., p. 108.

43. Janet Flanner, speech to American Institute of Arts and Letters, in the Flanner/Solano papers of the Library of Congress, n.d.

EPILOGUE

1. Janet Flanner, "Paris, Germany," *The New Yorker* (7 December 1940), reprinted in Janet Flanner, *Janet Flanner's World: Uncollected Writings 1932–1975* (New York and London: Harcourt Brace Jovanovich, 1979), p. 51.

2. Adrienne Monnier, "Occupation Journal: May 8 to July 10,1940," *The Very Rich Hours of Adrienne Monnier* (New York: Charles Scribner's Sons, 1976), p. 394.

3. Colette, quoted in Herbert Lottman, *Colette: A Life* (London: Secker and Warburg, 1991), p. 240.

4. Colette, "Fifteen hundred days: liberation, August 1944," *Earthly Paradise: Colette's Autobiography, drawn from the writings of her lifetime* by Robert Phelps (New York: Farrar, Straus and Giroux, 1966), p. 458.

5. Nancy Cunard, quoted in Anne Chisholm, *Nancy Cunard* (London: Sidgwick & Jackson, 1979), p. 263.

6. Shari Benstock, *Women of the Left Bank* (Austin: University of Texas Press, 1986 and London: Virago Press, 1987), p. 140.

7. Bryher, "For Sylvia," *Sylvia Beach: 1887–1962* (Paris: Mercure de France, 1963), p. 18.

8. Alice B. Toklas to W.G. Rogers, 28 October 1947, published in Edward Burns, ed., *Staying on Alone: Letters of Alice B. Toklas* (New York: Vintage Books, 1975), p. 88.

9. Alice B. Toklas to Henry Rago, 16 March 1947, published in Edward Burns, ed., *Staying on Alone: Letters of Alice B. Toklas,* ibid., p. 57.

10. Djuna Barnes to Solita Solano, 7 September 1960, Flanner/Solano papers, Library of Congress.

11. Djuna Barnes to Solita Solano, 22 May 1964, Flanner/Solano papers, Library of Congress.

SELECTED BIBLIOGRAPHY

Adams, Bronte and Trudi Tate, eds., *That Kind of Woman: Stories from the Left Bank and Beyond.* London: Virago, 1991.

Barnes, Djuna, *Nightwood.* London and Boston: Faber and Faber, 1985.

Beach, Sylvia, *Shakespeare and Company.* New York: Harcourt Brace and Company, 1959.

Benstock, Shari., *Women of the Left Bank.* Austin: University of Texas Press, 1986.

Broe, Mary Lynn, ed., *Silence and Power: A Reevaluation of Djuna Barnes.* Carbondale: Southern Illinois University Press, 1991.

Bryher, *The Heart to Artemis.* London: Collins, 1963.

Colette, *The Pure and the Impure.* Translation by Herma Briffault, introduction by Janet Flanner. London: Penguin Books, 1971.

Fitch, Noel Riley, *Sylvia Beach and the Lost Generation.* New York and London: W.W. Norton & Co., 1983.

Flanner, Janet, *Paris Was Yesterday, 1925-1939.* New York and London: Harcourt Brace Jovanovich, 1988.

Grahn, Judy, *Really Reading Gertrude Stein.* Freedom, California: The Crossing Press, 1989.

Jay, Karla, *The Amazon and the Page: Natalie Clifford Barney and Renée Vivien.* Bloomington: Indiana University Press, 1988.

Monnier, Adrienne, *The Very Rich Hours of Adrienne Monnier.* Translation and introduction by Richard McDougall. New York: Charles Scribner's Sons, 1976.

Stendhal, Renata, *Gertrude Stein in Words and Pictures.* London: Thames and Hudson, 1995.

Stimpson, Catharine R., "Gertrice/Altrude: Stein, Toklas, and the Paradox of the Happy Marriage." In Perry, Ruth, and Martine Watson Brownley, eds. *Mothering the Mind: Twelve Studies of Writers and Their Silent Partners.* New York and London: Holmes and Meier, 1984.

Wickes, George, *The Amazons of Letters.* New York: G.P Putnam's Sons, 1976.

Wineapple, Brenda, *Genêt: A Biography of Janet Flanner.* New York: Ticknor and Fields, 1989, and London: Pandora, 1993.

Photo and Text Credits

Permission to publish photographic and other visual work in this book has kindly been granted by the following sources:

Archives and Manuscripts, McKeldin Library, University of Maryland at College Park: pages xx, 108, 110, 111, 113, 114, 116, 119, 122, 124, 126, 129, 130, 131, 132, 134, 137, 176.

The Baltimore Museum of Art: The Cone Collection, formed by Dr. Claribel Cone and Miss Etta Cone of Baltimore, Maryland: page 51.

Bancroft Library, University of California at Berkeley: pages 37, 56, 58.

The Beinecke Rare Book and Manuscript Library, Yale University: pages 10, 32, 41, 42, 44, 46, 63, 125, 151 (© Man Ray), 168, 171.

Department of Rare Books and Special Collections, Princeton University Libraries: pages xxx, xxxii, 2, 4, 6, 15, 16, 18, 22, 24, 26, 28, 31, 169, 186, 191, 19.

The Estate of Carl Van Vechten, courtesy of Joseph Solomon, Executor: pages xxix, 34, 60, 112, 194.

The Estate of Janet Flanner, courtesy of William B. Murray: page 64.

Fonds Littéraire Jacques Doucet: pages 8, 52, 70, 71, 73, 75, 76, 82, 85, 87, 92, 97, 104, 107.

Gisèle Freund: pages xxii, 13, 21.

Smithsonian American Art Museum, Washington DC (Gift of the artist): 72, 74, 91, 100.

The Poetry Collection of the University Libraries, University at Buffalo, The State University of New York: page xviii.

Prints and Photographs Division, Library of Congress: 79, 98. 140, 142, 143, 144, 145, 146 , 152 (© Berenice Abbott), 154, 156 (courtesy of World Wide Photos), 160, 161, 162, 172, 175, 179, 180, 182, 183, 184, 188, 189, 192, 196.

Books and articles quoted or cited in the text under the usual fair use allowances are acknowledged in the endnotes. For more extensive quotations and to quote from unpublished material, I wish to thank the following sources:

The Estate of Gertrude Stein for permission to quote extracts from the published and unpublished writings by Gertrude Stein, and Random House for permission to reprint selections from *Four Saints in Three Acts, The Autobiography of Alice B. Toklas, Everybody's Autobiography,* and *Wars I Have Seen.* The Estate of Sylvia Beach, courtesy of Frederic B. Dennis, for permission to quote from her unpublished letters. The Estate of Mina Loy, courtesy of Roger L. Conover, for permission to reprint Mina Loy's poem 'Gertrude Stein.' The Estate of Natalie Clifford Barney, courtesy of François Chapon, for permission to publish extracts from Natalie Barney's autobiography and letters. The Authors League Fund, New York, and the Historic Churches Preservation Trust, London, for permission to quote from *Ladies*

Almanack, Nightwood, and from the letters of Djuna Barnes. Liveright Publishing Corporation for permission to quote from *Staying On Alone: Letters of Alice B. Toklas.* The Estates of H.D. and Bryher, courtesy of Perdita Schaffner, for permission to publish extracts from their letters, and the Estate of Janet Flanner, courtesy of William B. Murray, for permission to quote from *Paris Was Yesterday* and from unpublished writings by Janet Flanner.

Every effort has been made to trace the copyright holders of material reprinted in this book. The author and publisher respectfully request that any copyright holder not listed here contact the publisher so that due acknowledgement may appear in subsequent editions.

ABOUT THE AUTHOR

ANDREA WEISS is an award-winning documentary filmmaker and nonfiction author with a PhD in History. Her most recent book, *In the Shadow of the Magic Mountain: The Erika and Klaus Mann Story,* won the Publishing Triangle Award for nonfiction, and *Paris Was a Woman* won the Lambda Literary Award when it was first published. She received an Emmy for her documentary film *Before Stonewall.*

Weiss has been awarded fellowships from the National Endowment for the Humanities, National Endowment for the Arts, New York State Council on the Arts, and New York Foundation for the Arts. She was Artist-in-Residence at the Banff Center for the Arts, the Atlantic Center for the Arts, and the D.A.A.D. Artist Program in Berlin. A native New Yorker, she has lived in London, Berlin, and Barcelona, and currently is a professor of film/video at the City College of New York.

AVAILABLE ON DVD

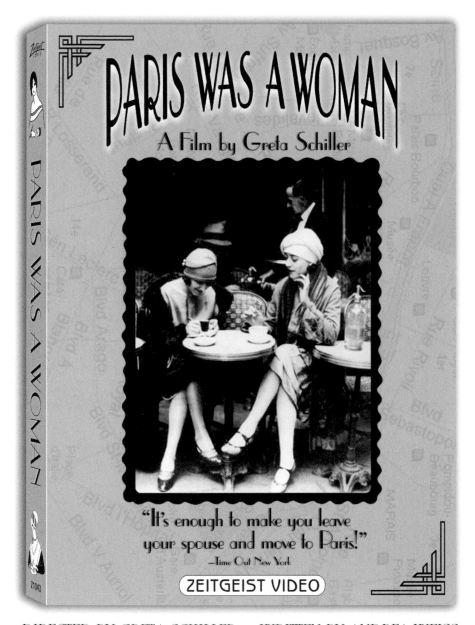

DIRECTED BY GRETA SCHILLER • WRITTEN BY ANDREA WEISS

'Time travel to golden ages doesn't exist, but documentaries like PARIS WAS A WOMAN are the next best thing."
—*The New York Times*

DVD SPECIAL FEATURES INCLUDE:

• Rare home movies of Gertrude Stein, Alice B. Toklas, Colette, Pablo Picasso and more
• Additional interviews illuminating connections between Hemingway, Stein and James Joyce
Archival photo gallery of the period • Biographies of the filmmakers and selected film subjects

AVAILABLE TO PURCHASE FROM **www.zeitgeistfilms.com**